In bringing together the best of Edwin Arlington Robinson's Tilbury Town poems, Lawrance Thompson has formed an illuminating critical sixty-three dramatic portraits terizations, soliloquies, dialogu narratives, have hitherto been iso scattered through more than 1400 pages of Robinson's *Collected Poems*. Here, for the first time, these separate pieces are shown as interacting and merging to create a Human Comedy, integrated not only through a common setting but also through a dominant theme.

TILBURY TOWN

Dear friends, reproach me not for what I do,
Nor counsel me, nor pity me; nor say
That I am wearing half my life away
For bubble-work that only fools pursue.
And if my bubbles be too small for you,
Blow bigger then your own: the games we play
To fill the frittered minutes of a day,
Good glasses are to read the spirit through.

And whoso reads may get him some shrewd skill;
And some unprofitable scorn resign,
To praise the very thing that he deplores;
So, friends (dear friends), remember, if you will,
The shame I win for singing is all mine,
The gold I miss for dreaming is all yours.

TILBURY TOWN

SELECTED POEMS OF
EDWIN ARLINGTON ROBINSON

Introduction and Notes
by LAWRANCE THOMPSON

THE MACMILLAN COMPANY

NEW YORK 1953

First Printing.

Printed in the United States of America
by The Haddon Craftsmen, Inc., Scranton, Pa.

CONTENTS

Introduction   ix

I: PREDICAMENTS

Flammonde	3
Miniver Cheevy	6
Old King Cole	8
Aaron Stark	11
Cassandra	12
Lost Anchors	14
Fragment	15
Aunt Imogen	16
The Long Race	21
The Dark House	22
Cliff Klingenhagen	24
Fleming Helphenstine	25
Bokardo	26
The Poor Relation	30
Theophilus	33
Uncle Ananias	34
Bewick Finzer	35
Siege Perilous	36
The Voice of Age	37
Richard Cory	38
An Evangelist's Wife	39
Vickery's Mountain	40
The Tree in Pamela's Garden	42

II: PASSIONS

The Story of the Ashes and the Flame   45
Her Eyes   46
Reuben Bright   48
Job the Rejected   49
Firelight   50
Ben Trovato   51
The Gift of God   52
Vain Gratuities   54
The Companion   55
The Clinging Vine   56
The Growth of "Lorraine"   59
Llewellyn and the Tree   60
Another Dark Lady   65
The Unforgiven   66
Eros Turannos   68
Luke Havergal   70

III: THE DEAD

A Man in Our Town   73
Exit   74
Amaryllis   75
Charles Carville's Eyes   76
Souvenir   77
Hector Kane   78
For a Dead Lady   81
The Whip   82
The Mill   84
The Rat   85
Inferential   86
Leonora   87
How Annandale Went Out   88
Annandale Again   89
Supremacy   96

IV: EDGE OF TOWN

John Evereldown 99
The Tavern 100
The House on the Hill 101
Mr. Flood's Party 102
Isaac and Archibald 104
Archibald's Example 116
Recalled 117
Stafford's Cabin 118
The Sheaves 119
New England 120

V: AGAINST THE SKY

The Man Against the Sky 123

Notes 133
Index 144

INTRODUCTION

ONE high tribute which we pay quite unconsciously to the poetic art of Edwin Arlington Robinson is that many of us know some of these Tilbury Town poems by heart without ever having tried to memorize them. Hitherto isolated and scattered through some fourteen hundred pages of Robinson's *Collected Poems*, these familiar faces have always seemed to lean toward each other, talk to each other, explain each other, even gossip about each other. They belong together, and this critical act of bringing the best of them together is intended as a further tribute to Robinson's various artistic skills.

We naturally remember these Tilbury Town poems as many-sided. If we start by calling them stories-in-verse we are never far wrong because each contains some qualities of narrative, mixed with subtle qualities of song. If we go on to say that their flavor recalls the bitter-sweet tang of a firm Down East apple we do no injustice to the universality of their appeal. If we take them as terse and elliptical probings into obscure psychological motivations we again include most of them. If we remember some of them as miniature poetic scenes in the larger Tilbury Town drama, we honor an essentially dramatic element in them all. But first and last our pleasure is to enjoy them for the peculiar felicity of Robinson's utterance, for the ironically witty turns of word and phrase, for the apt rhythms and cadences of the lines, and for the cunningly varied structures which give new vitality to old verse forms.

As soon as we notice that most of these poems are explicitly or implicitly integrated by the gathering metaphor of the Tilbury Town backdrop or setting, we quickly discover that three different tensions of interest are evoked, poetically and dramatically; that at least three different kinds of conflict are interwoven. At first glance we are aware of the obvious conflicts within or between these imagined characters whom Robinson has brought to life in or on the edge of Tilbury Town. A second glance makes us feel that most of these characters are represented as being in conflict with the prudent and conventional morality of Tilbury Town, where the group tends to pass relentless judgment on all misfits and failures who find themselves at odds with the money-conscious worship of material success. A third glance is not necessary to make us realize that the poet-as-observer, standing apart from the Tilbury Town group, on the one hand, and from the isolated individuals, on the other hand, shows an open hostility toward the Tilbury Town group and shows sympathetic compassion for the misfits, the failures, the disappointed. Because any single one of these conflicts would be adequate for purposes of poetic and dramatic narrative, we enjoy this rich interplay of conflicts as sheer poetic luxury.

Yet our pleasures are increased when we notice the consistency with which Robinson makes use of sly wit and wry humour to keep his double-edged response under artistic control and balance. The majority of the human predicaments here described are essentially tragic or at least pathetic, and the danger was that Robinson's deep compassion might have gotten out of hand. It never does, I think, and one kind of pleasure available to us is to notice the variety of ways in which he avoids this pitfall. Detachment is implicit in the essentially dramatic role of the poet-as-observer; but the beauty of that detachment, artistically considered, becomes most apparent only after we have let the poet sensitize our ears to those extraordinary modulations of tone which he somehow manages to catch and imprison through his skillful and cunning arrangements of words. His most oblique comments on either the misfits or the ostracizing group are conveyed through mere nuances of tone which range through ironic wit, playfulness, teasing, smiling, indulgence, tenderness, pity, sarcasm, bitterness, scorn, together with all the possible permutations and combinations. Yet always, beneath or through the usually gentle spirit of his human comedy (which for Robinson is one type of tragedy), the poet invites us to join him in refusing to pass quick judgments against the actions of his isolated characters in or on the edge of Tilbury Town.

All the technical factors which I have mentioned, so far, are utilized concurrently by Robinson as a complex means to the end of illuminating his own scale of values and his ulterior conceptual concerns. Indirectly and variously, he concentrates our attention on dramatized evidence that no human errors, disappointments, failures, need be viewed as destroying the wellsprings of human dignity or crippling the potentials of spiritual self-realization. Again and again he finds symbolic ways for suggesting that many of his isolated individuals have learned how to translate different forms of hurt and loss into perceptions which somehow compensate for hurt and loss.

Yet he goes even deeper to hint that his most persistent probings beneath the surface of either the tragic or the pathetic are performed to intensify his and our awareness of that which remains unknown and unknowable in the human predicament. His kind of poetic hesitation, on the verge of discovery and revelation, seems offered repeatedly as an implicit corrective for the cocksure faultfinding of the Tilbury Town group, which is always inclined to insist that there is no mystery about human action; that the individual who fails is somehow to blame for whatever happens.

As soon as we are aware of the extensions of meaning made available to us through the poet's double-edged attitude toward the town and the isolated individuals, we can advance one step further in our enjoyment of certain symbolic meanings implicit in the structures of these poems. Robinson has frequently been criticized for achieving surface effects of obscurity, uncertainty, vagueness; but this would seem to be a risk he deliberately took. If the modes and structures of these separate pieces occasionally perplex those who insist that poetry should begin and end with vivid concrete imagery; if Robinson's brooding manner may seem to involve too often the blurred, the puzzling, the elliptical, perhaps we may find that this aspect of his art is justified because it helps him dramatize and illuminate a recurrent theme. Repeatedly he invites the reader to linger over baffling actions or situations which suggest several possibilities of explanation, but which admit no certainties of explanation. Perhaps it could be said that Robinson uses his compressed idiom to require such deliberate and thoughtful progression that we have no choice: we must read closely, slowly, hesitatingly, cautiously, wonderingly, if we are to comprehend even the specific details of the

surface meaning. As we perform that necessary process of close reading and contemplation and reconsideration, perhaps it dawns on us that
we ourselves are thus acting out an important aspect of the poet's
meaning.

An illustration may be in order here. Consider what happens to us
when we confront and are confronted by that cryptically inferential
fragment of a story entitled "The Whip." If we could remember our
first reading of it, probably all of us would confess that we reached the
end of those five tight octaves with a disturbed sense of bafflement as
to whether even a surface meaning had been adequately realized by the
poet. Although our understanding of "The Whip" may have increased
with each successive reading, we admit that we have not yet resolved
and removed our initial sense of perplexity. Isn't it possible that the
poet had a particular purpose in mind, when he created that effect?
In retrospect, we remember a few specifics which can be summarized
briefly. The immediate situation represents the poet-observer as mus-
ing over an open casket which contains the body of an acquaintance
who has recently drowned himself. Meditatively, and yet with the
slightest hint of irony in his voice, the poet conducts a necessarily one-
sided conversation with the dead man in an attempt to find an answer
to the obvious question: why did he do it? But the circumstantial evidence, stated or guessed, in the poet's soliloquy merely heightens his
(and our) sense of perplexity. From the evidence poetically given us,
we tell ourselves cautiously that this dead man's troubles seem to
have stemmed from an inner conflict involving his doubts as to whether
his wife had always been faithful to him. But the poem starts with something more than a hint at this inner conflict:

> "The doubt you fought so long,
> The cynic net you cast . . ."

In the total context provided by the poem, there are several hints that
the dead man had seemed anxious to prove the truth of his suspicion,
cynically, and almost as though he would have been somehow disappointed if his suspicion had not been true. In this sense, the title seems
to pick up a first metaphorical extension: the husband may have used
his doubt as a whip. Whether or not he ever caught any proofs in his
"cynic net," we are not told; but late in the poem we gather that on

the last day of his life he became involved in an absurd horseback chase after the wife and the man suspected as lover, riding together in full view of the pursuer; that as the husband overtook them, the wife turned and struck him across the face with her crop or whip. This little symbolic action the poet half guesses because of a curious welt he notices on the face of the dead man. Poetically considered, the images of the welt and the whip would seem to invite the reader beneath the surface of appearances and actions to speculate concerning the motives of both husband and wife. "Doubt" is obliquely represented as having caused certain blind spots in the husband's vision. But if blind to love, the poet wonders, would wounded pride be an adequate motive for suicide? Or is it possible that his own perception of some analogy between his doubting, and her striking with the whip, may have cured one of his blind spots and restored one kind of vision? Perhaps, at the end, he was not so blind as his neighbors thought. Is it possible that his suicide might be considered as a kind of recognition-scene? All these questions are suggested by the poet's brooding speculation, and although he is not certain as to motives, his questionings have evoked in him (and in us) enough compassion to restrain fault-finding judgments against either the husband or the wife who struck with a whip.

This is only one possible interpretation of the poem, and I give it merely to suggest Robinson's way of using poetic structure, and of requiring close reading of us, to let us act out an important aspect of his sub-surface meaning. Whenever we do follow him below appearances into the darkly mysterious realm of complex psychological mystery, those of us who seek clarified and simplified meanings are likely to find ourselves in company with the disappointed guest who visited Old King Cole:

> And once a man was there all night,
> Expecting something every minute.

In reading any of these tantalizing poems, perhaps our greatest surprise and pleasure is evoked by our ultimate discovery that Robinson manages to pass enough whole light of psychological consciousness through the immediate prism of his poetry to refract a few colors with sharpness and brilliancy. Notice also that the immediate prism is ingeniously created through the pertinently intricate interplay of words, phrases, rhythms, verse forms, all of which contribute something to the total effect. After we have recognized the peculiar nature of the prosodic difficulties which Robinson boldly set for himself, in some of his poems, and then so gracefully overcame, we return to this aspect of his artistry with heightened admiration.

Robinson's extraordinary technical cunning was earned during long years of painstaking practice and experiment, while he waited for recognition. He was forced to develop patience of at least two kinds because, during those apprentice years spent in his home town of Gardiner, Maine, he suffered constantly from what he felt to be the hostility of many hard-headed Yankee townspeople toward such a seemingly shiftless occupation. Gardiner, a thriving river-town on the Kennebec, bustled so earnestly with enterprise and money-making that most of its citizens were impatient with anything that could not be translated into dollars and cents. Hence there is no difficulty in understanding why Robinson chose to embody in his imagined Tilbury Town some of those tensions and conflicts which he felt in his mingled love and hate for his down-Maine New England heritage.

While still trying to discover his own idiom, poetically and spiritually, he watched three other members of his family achieve material success. His father crowned a prosperous business career by becoming a director in two Gardiner banks. His older brother Herman made himself locally famous as a shrewd financial investor and then courted and married the loveliest girl in town. His still older brother Dean carried out medical training at Bowdoin and then began practice as a promising physician. On the streets of Gardiner, neighbors stopped this mere poet and observer to ask reprovingly, "And what are you going to do with yourself, Win?" It would have sounded silly if he had told them the truth. After having spent only two years at Harvard he had returned to Gardiner and had settled down at home to do nothing but write, write, write. Gradually his neighbors stopped enquiring, and merely implied the question in reproachful side-glances.

Life's Little Ironies was the wry title of a Hardy story which Robinson discovered and enjoyed reading, during these days. All too soon he endowed the phrase with personal and first-hand meanings. Just when he feared that he himself might prove to be a failure even in his own eyes, the health of his vigorous and prosperous father collapsed so frighteningly that he became a burdensome invalid in the home. A little later, his two brothers returned home as different kinds of failure. His brother Dean subsequently killed himself. Further biographical details are unnecessary, here. Enough for us to know that under his own roof in Gardiner, Maine, Robinson found abundant cause for brooding over questions as to how one should define and evaluate the ulterior meanings of disappointments, disgrace, failure. His desire to defend his brothers and himself against criticism heightened his impatience with the smugly Puritanical conventionalism of his non-artistic model for Tilbury Town, and his bitterness found vent of the sort reflected in the following letter to a former Harvard classmate, written three years before the appearance of Robinson's first (privately printed) book of poems:

"Gardiner is a small place, relatively, but it contains a good deal of weather at certain seasons of the year. In the past week—ever since my return from Cambridge—the place has been a frozen hell to me. Here I am, shut in by myself with only one or two people in town that I care two snaps of my fingers for (and who, in turn, care about as much for me) with no prospects except of the most shadowy nature, and hardly enough interest in the general political scheme of things to work out interest at six percent without cudgelling my brain more than I should over a proposition in Bokardo. I do not mean to say that I consider myself totally an ass (though they may) but merely that I lack a general interest in the practical side of things that may play the devil with my progress in this little journey to God knows where, which we are all making just now. I am afflicted with a kind of foolish pride that stands in my way every day of my life and which I am continually making heroic efforts to kick out. But it is 'no go.' I keep as much as I began with and if I end up a penniless *gent* full of golden theories of fame and riches I shall not lay all the blame, if there be blame in the matter, to myself; I shall not feel that it all might have been different, had I changed my opinions and actions a little when my mind was young and flexible. My philosophy does not swallow this teaching of our good old grandfathers who worked sixteen hours and sang psalms and praised heaven that a life is what we make it. And let me beg here that you may not permit any of your ambitious pupils to write essays on 'Every man the architect of his own fortune.'"

Deeply hurt, during those early years in Gardiner, Robinson gradually completed his self-assigned task of self-discovery and went on to use his poetry in part for purposes of self-defense and in part for purposes of self-justification. His wound, like Mercutio's, might seem trivial to others; but it would do. Sardonically he phrased another aspect of his discovery to one of his friends thus: "There's a good deal to live for, but a man has to go through hell really to find it out." What he found out, painfully, gave sharpness of color and phrasing and feeling and thought to the happy-sad music of all his poetry, particularly to his Tilbury Town poems.

The autobiographical aspects of the Tilbury Town poems are obviously of least importance. All we need remember, here, is that Robinson, while making continued use of the raw materials provided by his own experience, gradually learned more and more about the values of dramatically projecting his own personal perceptions through objective characterizations and portrayals of the human heart in conflict with itself. His own deeply cultivated sense of New England reticence and decorum must have helped him transmute his particular and private viewpoint into a genuinely classic and universal quality of poetic statement, which pictures afresh the old-new truths concerning inseparably tangled joys and sorrows, inextricably meshed good and evil, as viewed against the contrasted background of those Tilbury Town prejudices and assumptions which sort out all values in terms of either black or white. These poems represent his highest artistic achievement: they have earned him a well-deserved and distinguished position among our best American authors.

I

PREDICAMENTS

"Whether all towns and all who live in them
Are more or less the same, I leave to you."
"TASKER NORCROSS"

"The more we measure what is ours to use,
The less we groan for what the gods refuse."
"CAPTAIN CRAIG"

Flammonde

THE man Flammonde, from God knows where,
With firm address and foreign air,
With news of nations in his talk
And something royal in his walk,
With glint of iron in his eyes,
But never doubt, nor yet surprise,
Appeared, and stayed, and held his head
As one by kings accredited.

Erect, with his alert repose
About him, and about his clothes,
He pictured all tradition hears
Of what we owe to fifty years.
His cleansing heritage of taste
Paraded neither want nor waste;
And what he needed for his fee
To live, he borrowed graciously.

He never told us what he was,
Or what mischance, or other cause,
Had banished him from better days
To play the Prince of Castaways.
Meanwhile he played surpassing well
A part, for most, unplayable;
In fine, one pauses, half afraid
To say for certain that he played.

For that, one may as well forego
Conviction as to yes or no;
Nor can I say just how intense
Would then have been the difference
To several, who, having striven
In vain to get what he was given,
Would see the stranger taken on
By friends not easy to be won.

Moreover, many a malcontent
He soothed and found munificent;
His courtesy beguiled and foiled
Suspicion that his years were soiled;
His mien distinguished any crowd,
His credit strengthened when he bowed;
And women, young and old, were fond
Of looking at the man Flammonde.

There was a woman in our town
On whom the fashion was to frown;
But while our talk renewed the tinge
Of a long-faded scarlet fringe,
The man Flammonde saw none of that,
And what he saw we wondered at—
That none of us, in her distress,
Could hide or find our littleness.

There was a boy that all agreed
Had shut within him the rare seed
Of learning. We could understand,
But none of us could lift a hand.
The man Flammonde appraised the youth,
And told a few of us the truth;
And thereby, for a little gold,
A flowered future was unrolled.

There were two citizens who fought
For years and years, and over nought;
They made life awkward for their friends,
And shortened their own dividends.
The man Flammonde said what was wrong
Should be made right; nor was it long
Before they were again in line,
And had each other in to dine.

And these I mention are but four
Of many out of many more.
So much for them. But what of him—
So firm in every look and limb?
What small satanic sort of kink
Was in his brain? What broken link
Withheld him from the destinies
That came so near to being his?

What was he, when we came to sift
His meaning, and to note the drift
Of incommunicable ways
That make us ponder while we praise?
Why was it that his charm revealed
Somehow the surface of a shield?
What was it that we never caught?
What was he, and what was he not?

How much it was of him we met
We cannot ever know; nor yet
Shall all he gave us quite atone
For what was his, and his alone;
Nor need we now, since he knew best,
Nourish an ethical unrest:
Rarely at once will nature give
The power to be Flammonde and live.

We cannot know how much we learn
From those who never will return,
Until a flash of unforeseen
Remembrance falls on what has been.
We've each a darkening hill to climb;
And this is why, from time to time
In Tilbury Town, we look beyond
Horizons for the man Flammonde.

Miniver Cheevy

MINIVER CHEEVY, child of scorn,
  Grew lean while he assailed the seasons;
He wept that he was ever born,
  And he had reasons.

Miniver loved the days of old
  When swords were bright and steeds were prancing;
The vision of a warrior bold
  Would set him dancing.

Miniver sighed for what was not,
  And dreamed, and rested from his labors;
He dreamed of Thebes and Camelot,
  And Priam's neighbors.

Miniver mourned the ripe renown
  That made so many a name so fragrant;
He mourned Romance, now on the town,
  And Art, a vagrant.

Miniver loved the Medici,
  Albeit he had never seen one;
He would have sinned incessantly
  Could he have been one.

Miniver cursed the commonplace
  And eyed a khaki suit with loathing;
He missed the mediæval grace
  Of iron clothing.

Miniver scorned the gold he sought,
  But sore annoyed was he without it;
Miniver thought, and thought, and thought,
  And thought about it.

Miniver Cheevy, born too late,
   Scratched his head and kept on thinking;
Miniver coughed, and called it fate,
   And kept on drinking.

Old King Cole

In Tilbury Town did Old King Cole
A wise old age anticipate,
Desiring, with his pipe and bowl,
No Khan's extravagant estate.
No crown annoyed his honest head,
No fiddlers three were called or needed;
For two disastrous heirs instead
Made music more than ever three did.

Bereft of her with whom his life
Was harmony without a flaw,
He took no other for a wife,
Nor sighed for any that he saw;
And if he doubted his two sons,
And heirs, Alexis and Evander,
He might have been as doubtful once
Of Robert Burns and Alexander.

Alexis, in his early youth,
Began to steal—from old and young.
Likewise Evander, and the truth
Was like a bad taste on his tongue.
Born thieves and liars, their affair
Seemed only to be tarred with evil—
The most insufferable pair
Of scamps that ever cheered the devil.

The world went on, their fame went on,
And they went on—from bad to worse;
Till, goaded hot with nothing done,
And each accoutred with a curse,
The friends of Old King Cole, by twos,
And fours, and sevens, and elevens,
Pronounced unalterable views
Of doings that were not of heaven's.

8

And having learned again whereby
Their baleful zeal had come about,
King Cole met many a wrathful eye
So kindly that its wrath went out—
Or partly out. Say what they would,
He seemed the more to court their candor;
But never told what kind of good
Was in Alexis and Evander.

And Old King Cole, with many a puff
That haloed his urbanity,
Would smoke till he had smoked enough,
And listen most attentively.
He beamed as with an inward light
That had the Lord's assurance in it;
And once a man was there all night,
Expecting something every minute.

But whether from too little thought,
Or too much fealty to the bowl,
A dim reward was all he got
For sitting up with Old King Cole.
"Though mine," the father mused aloud,
"Are not the sons I would have chosen,
Shall I, less evilly endowed,
By their infirmity be frozen?

"They'll have a bad end, I'll agree,
But I was never born to groan;
For I can see what I can see,
And I'm accordingly alone.
With open heart and open door,
I love my friends, I like my neighbors;
But if I try to tell you more,
Your doubts will overmatch my labors.

"This pipe would never make me calm,
This bowl my grief would never drown.
For grief like mine there is no balm
In Gilead, or in Tilbury Town.
And if I see what I can see,
I know not any way to blind it;
Nor more if any way may be
For you to grope or fly to find it.

"There may be room for ruin yet,
And ashes for a wasted love;
Or, like One whom you may forget,
I may have meat you know not of.
And if I'd rather live than weep
Meanwhile, do you find that surprising?
Why, bless my soul, the man's asleep!
That's good. The sun will soon be rising."

Aaron Stark

WITHAL a meagre man was Aaron Stark,
Cursed and unkempt, shrewd, shrivelled, and morose.
A miser was he, with a miser's nose,
And eyes like little dollars in the dark.
His thin, pinched mouth was nothing but a mark;
And when he spoke there came like sullen blows
Through scattered fangs a few snarled words and close,
As if a cur were chary of its bark.

Glad for the murmur of his hard renown,
Year after year he shambled through the town,
A loveless exile moving with a staff;
And oftentimes there crept into his ears
A sound of alien pity, touched with tears,—
And then (and only then) did Aaron laugh.

Cassandra

I HEARD one who said: "Verily,
  What word have I for children here?
Your Dollar is your only Word,
  The wrath of it your only fear.

"You build it altars tall enough
  To make you see, but you are blind;
You cannot leave it long enough
  To look before you or behind.

"When Reason beckons you to pause,
  You laugh and say that you know best;
But what it is you know, you keep
  As dark as ingots in a chest.

"You laugh and answer, 'We are young;
  O leave us now, and let us grow.'—
Not asking how much more of this
  Will Time endure or Fate bestow.

"Because a few complacent years
  Have made your peril of your pride,
Think you that you are to go on
  Forever pampered and untried?

"What lost eclipse of history,
  What bivouac of the marching stars,
Has given the sign for you to see
  Millenniums and last great wars?

"What unrecorded overthrow
  Of all the world has ever known,
Or ever been, has made itself
  So plain to you, and you alone?

"Your Dollar, Dove and Eagle make
  A Trinity that even you
Rate higher than you rate yourselves;
  It pays, it flatters, and it's new.

"And though your very flesh and blood
  Be what your Eagle eats and drinks,
You'll praise him for the best of birds,
  Not knowing what the Eagle thinks.

"The power is yours, but not the sight;
  You see not upon what you tread;
You have the ages for your guide,
  But not the wisdom to be led.

"Think you to tread forever down
  The merciless old verities?
And are you never to have eyes
  To see the world for what it is?

"Are you to pay for what you have
  With all you are?"—No other word
We caught, but with a laughing crowd
  Moved on. None heeded, and few heard.

Lost Anchors

LIKE a dry fish flung inland far from shore,
There lived a sailor, warped and ocean-browned.
Who told of an old vessel, harbor-drowned
And out of mind a century before,
Where divers, on descending to explore
A legend that had lived its way around
The world of ships, in the dark hulk had found
Anchors, which had been seized and seen no more.

Improving a dry leisure to invest
Their misadventure with a manifest
Analogy that he may read who runs,
The sailor made it old as ocean grass—
Telling of much that once had come to pass
With him, whose mother should have had no sons.

Fragment

FAINT white pillars that seem to fade
As you look from here are the first one sees
Of his house where it hides and dies in a shade
Of beeches and oaks and hickory trees.
Not many a man, given woods like these,
And a house like that, and the Briony gold,
Would have said, "There are still some gods to please,
And houses are built without hands, we're told."

There are the pillars, and all gone gray.
Briony's hair went white. You may see
Where the garden was if you come this way.
That sun-dial scared him, he said to me;
"Sooner or later they strike," said he,
And he never got that from the books he read.
Others are flourishing, worse than he,
But he knew too much for the life he led.

And who knows all knows everything
That a patient ghost at last retrieves;
There's more to be known of his harvesting
When Time the thresher unbinds the sheaves;
And there's more to be heard than a wind that grieves
For Briony now in this ageless oak,
Driving the first of its withered leaves
Over the stones where the fountain broke.

Aunt Imogen

Aunt Imogen was coming, and therefore
The children—Jane, Sylvester, and Young George—
Were eyes and ears; for there was only one
Aunt Imogen to them in the whole world,
And she was in it only for four weeks
In fifty-two. But those great bites of time
Made all September a Queen's Festival;
And they would strive, informally, to make
The most of them.—The mother understood,
And wisely stepped away. Aunt Imogen
Was there for only one month in the year,
While she, the mother,—she was always there;
And that was what made all the difference.
She knew it must be so, for Jane had once
Expounded it to her so learnedly
That she had looked away from the child's eyes
And thought; and she had thought of many things.

There was a demonstration every time
Aunt Imogen appeared, and there was more
Than one this time. And she was at a loss
Just how to name the meaning of it all:
It puzzled her to think that she could be
So much to any crazy thing alive—
Even to her sister's little savages
Who knew no better than to be themselves;
But in the midst of her glad wonderment
She found herself besieged and overcome
By two tight arms and one tumultuous head,
And therewith half bewildered and half pained
By the joy she felt and by the sudden love
That proved itself in childhood's honest noise.
Jane, by the wings of sex, had reached her first;
And while she strangled her, approvingly,
Sylvester thumped his drum and Young George howled.

But finally, when all was rectified,
And she had stilled the clamor of Young George
By giving him a long ride on her shoulders,
They went together into the old room
That looked across the fields; and Imogen
Gazed out with a girl's gladness in her eyes,
Happy to know that she was back once more
Where there were those who knew her, and at last
Had gloriously got away again
From cabs and clattered asphalt for a while;
And there she sat and talked and looked and laughed
And made the mother and the children laugh.
Aunt Imogen made everybody laugh.

There was the feminine paradox—that she
Who had so little sunshine for herself
Should have so much for others. How it was
That she could make, and feel for making it,
So much of joy for them, and all along
Be covering, like a scar, and while she smiled,
That hungering incompleteness and regret—
That passionate ache for something of her own,
For something of herself—she never knew.
She knew that she could seem to make them all
Believe there was no other part of her
Than her persistent happiness; but the why
And how she did not know. Still none of them
Could have a thought that she was living down—
Almost as if regret were criminal,
So proud it was and yet so profitless—
The penance of a dream, and that was good.
Her sister Jane—the mother of little Jane,
Sylvester, and Young George—might make herself
Believe she knew, for she—well, she was Jane.

Young George, however, did not yield himself
To nourish the false hunger of a ghost
That made no good return. He saw too much:
The accumulated wisdom of his years
Had so conclusively made plain to him
The permanent profusion of a world
Where everybody might have everything
To do, and almost everything to eat,
That he was jubilantly satisfied
And all unthwarted by adversity.
Young George knew things. The world, he had found out,
Was a good place, and life was a good game—
Particularly when Aunt Imogen
Was in it. And one day it came to pass—
One rainy day when she was holding him
And rocking him—that he, in his own right,
Took it upon himself to tell her so;
And something in his way of telling it—
The language, or the tone, or something else—
Gripped like insidious fingers on her throat,
And then went foraging as if to make
A plaything of her heart. Such undeserved
And unsophisticated confidence
Went mercilessly home; and had she sat
Before a looking glass, the deeps of it
Could not have shown more clearly to her then
Than one thought-mirrored little glimpse had shown,
The pang that wrenched her face and filled her eyes
With anguish and intolerable mist.
The blow that she had vaguely thrust aside
Like fright so many times had found her now:
Clean-thrust and final it had come to her
From a child's lips at last, as it had come
Never before, and as it might be felt
Never again. Some grief, like some delight,
Stings hard but once: to custom after that
The rapture or the pain submits itself,

And we are wiser than we were before.
And Imogen was wiser; though at first
Her dream-defeating wisdom was indeed
A thankless heritage: there was no sweet,
No bitter now; nor was there anything
To make a daily meaning for her life—
Till truth, like Harlequin, leapt out somehow
From ambush and threw sudden savor to it—
But the blank taste of time. There were no dreams,
No phantoms in her future any more:
One clinching revelation of what was
One by-flash of irrevocable chance,
Had acridly but honestly foretold
The mystical fulfilment of a life
That might have once . . . But that was all gone by:
There was no need of reaching back for that:
The triumph was not hers: there was no love
Save borrowed love: there was no might have been.

But there was yet Young George—and he had gone
Conveniently to sleep, like a good boy;
And there was yet Sylvester with his drum,
And there was frowzle-headed little Jane;
And there was Jane the sister, and the mother,—
Her sister, and the mother of them all.
They were not hers, not even one of them:
She was not born to be so much as that,
For she was born to be Aunt Imogen.
Now she could see the truth and look at it;
Now she could make stars out where once had palled
A future's emptiness; now she could share
With others—ah, the others!—to the end
The largess of a woman who could smile;
Now it was hers to dance the folly down,
And all the murmuring; now it was hers
To be Aunt Imogen.—So, when Young George
Woke up and blinked at her with his big eyes,

And smiled to see the way she blinked at him,
'T was only in old concord with the stars
That she took hold of him and held him close,
Close to herself, and crushed him till he laughed.

The Long Race

Up the old hill to the old house again
Where fifty years ago the friend was young
Who should be waiting somewhere there among
Old things that least remembered most remain,
He toiled on with a pleasure that was pain
To think how soon asunder would be flung
The curtain half a century had hung
Between the two ambitions they had slain.

They dredged an hour for words, and then were done.
"Good-bye! . . . You have the same old weather-vane—
Your little horse that's always on the run."
And all the way down back to the next train,
Down the old hill to the old road again,
It seemed as if the little horse had won.

The Dark House

WHERE a faint light shines alone,
Dwells a Demon I have known.
Most of you had better say
"The Dark House," and go your way.
Do not wonder if I stay.

For I know the Demon's eyes,
And their lure that never dies.
Banish all your fond alarms,
For I know the foiling charms
Of her eyes and of her arms,

And I know that in one room
Burns a lamp as in a tomb;
And I see the shadow glide,
Back and forth, of one denied
Power to find himself outside.

There he is who is my friend,
Damned, he fancies, to the end—
Vanquished, ever since a door
Closed, he thought, for evermore
On the life that was before.

And the friend who knows him best
Sees him as he sees the rest
Who are striving to be wise
While a Demon's arms and eyes
Hold them as a web would flies.

All the words of all the world,
Aimed together and then hurled,
Would be stiller in his ears
Than a closing of still shears
On a thread made out of years.

But there lives another sound,
More compelling, more profound;
There's a music, so it seems,
That assuages and redeems,
More than reason, more than dreams.

There's a music yet unheard
By the creature of the word,
Though it matters little more
Than a wave-wash on a shore—
Till a Demon shuts a door.

So, if he be very still
With his Demon, and one will,
Murmurs of it may be blown
To my friend who is alone
In a room that I have known.

After that from everywhere
Singing life will find him there;
Then the door will open wide,
And my friend, again outside,
Will be living, having died.

Cliff Klingenhagen

CLIFF KLINGENHAGEN had me in to dine
With him one day; and after soup and meat,
And all the other things there were to eat,
Cliff took two glasses and filled one with wine
And one with wormwood. Then, without a sign
For me to choose at all, he took the draught
Of bitterness himself, and lightly quaffed
It off, and said the other one was mine.

And when I asked him what the deuce he meant
By doing that, he only looked at me
And smiled, and said it was a way of his.
And though I know the fellow, I have spent
Long time a-wondering when I shall be
As happy as Cliff Klingenhagen is.

Fleming Helphenstine

AT first I thought there was a superfine
Persuasion in his face; but the free glow
That filled it when he stopped and cried, "Hollo!"
Shone joyously, and so I let it shine.
He said his name was Fleming Helphenstine,
But be that as it may;—I only know
He talked of this and that and So-and-So,
And laughed and chaffed like any friend of mine.

But soon, with a queer, quick frown, he looked at me,
And I looked hard at him; and there we gazed
In a strained way that made us cringe and wince:
Then, with a wordless clogged apology
That sounded half confused and half amazed,
He dodged,—and I have never seen him since.

Bokardo

WELL, Bokardo, here we are;
　　Make yourself at home.
Look around—you haven't far
　　To look—and why be dumb?
Not the place that used to be,
Not so many things to see;
But there's room for you and me.
　　And you—you've come.

Talk a little; or, if not,
　　Show me with a sign
Why it was that you forgot
　　What was yours and mine.
Friends, I gather, are small things
In an age when coins are kings:
Even at that, one hardly flings
　　Friends before swine.

Rather strong? I knew as much,
　　For it made you speak.
No offense to swine, as such,
　　But why this hide-and-seek?
You have something on your side,
And you wish you might have died,
So you tell me. And you tried
　　One night last week?

You tried hard? And even then
　　Found a time to pause?
When you try as hard again,
　　You'll have another cause.
When you find yourself at odds
With all dreamers of all gods,
You may smite yourself with rods—
　　But not the laws.

26

Though they seem to show a spite
    Rather devilish,
They move on as with a might
    Stronger than your wish.
Still, however strong they be,
They bide man's authority:
Xerxes, when he flogged the sea,
    May've scared a fish.

It's a comfort, if you like,
    To keep honor warm,
But as often as you strike
    The laws, you do no harm.
To the laws, I mean. To you—
That's another point of view,
One you may as well indue
    With some alarm.

Not the most heroic face
    To present, I grant;
Nor will you insure disgrace
    By fearing what you want.
Freedom has a world of sides,
And if reason once derides
Courage, then your courage hides
    A deal of cant.

Learn a little to forget
    Life was once a feast;
You aren't fit for dying yet,
    So don't be a beast.
Few men with a mind will say,
Thinking twice, that they can pay
Half their debts of yesterday,
    Or be released.

There's a debt now on your mind
    More than any gold?
And there's nothing you can find
    Out there in the cold?
Only—what's his name?—Remorse?
And Death riding on his horse?
Well, be glad there's nothing worse
    Than you have told.

Leave Remorse to warm his hands
    Outside in the rain.
As for Death, he understands,
    And he will come again.
Therefore, till your wits are clear,
Flourish and be quiet—here.
But a devil at each ear
    Will be a strain?

Past a doubt they will indeed,
    More than you have earned.
I say that because you need
    Ablution, being burned?
Well, if you must have it so,
Your last flight went rather low.
Better say you had to know
    What you have learned.

And that's over. Here you are,
    Battered by the past.
Time will have his little scar,
    But the wound won't last.
Nor shall harrowing surprise
Find a world without its eyes
If a star fades when the skies
    Are overcast.

God knows there are lives enough,
   Crushed, and too far gone
Longer to make sermons of,
   And those we leave alone.
Others, if they will, may rend
The worn patience of a friend
Who, though smiling, sees the end,
   With nothing done.

But your fervor to be free
   Fled the faith it scorned;
Death demands a decency
   Of you, and you are warned.
But for all we give we get
Mostly blows? Don't be upset;
You, Bokardo, are not yet
   Consumed or mourned.

There'll be falling into view
   Much to rearrange;
And there'll be a time for you
   To marvel at the change.
They that have the least to fear
Question hardest what is here;
When long-hidden skies are clear,
   The stars look strange.

The Poor Relation

No longer torn by what she knows
And sees within the eyes of others,
Her doubts are when the daylight goes,
Her fears are for the few she bothers.
She tells them it is wholly wrong
Of her to stay alive so long;
And when she smiles her forehead shows
A crinkle that had been her mother's.

Beneath her beauty, blanched with pain,
And wistful yet for being cheated,
A child would seem to ask again
A question many times repeated;
But no rebellion has betrayed
Her wonder at what she has paid
For memories that have no stain,
For triumph born to be defeated.

To those who come for what she was—
The few left who know where to find her—
She clings, for they are all she has;
And she may smile when they remind her,
As heretofore, of what they know
Of roses that are still to blow
By ways where not so much as grass
Remains of what she sees behind her.

They stay a while, and having done
What penance or the past requires,
They go, and leave her there alone
To count her chimneys and her spires.
Her lip shakes when they go away,
And yet she would not have them stay;
She knows as well as anyone
That Pity, having played, soon tires.

But one friend always reappears,
A good ghost, not to be forsaken;
Whereat she laughs and has no fears
Of what a ghost may reawaken,
But welcomes, while she wears and mends
The poor relation's odds and ends,
Her truant from a tomb of years—
Her power of youth so early taken.

Poor laugh, more slender than her song
It seems; and there are none to hear it
With even the stopped ears of the strong
For breaking heart or broken spirit.
The friends who clamored for her place,
And would have scratched her for her face,
Have lost her laughter for so long
That none would care enough to fear it.

None live who need fear anything
From her, whose losses are their pleasure;
The plover with a wounded wing
Stays not the flight that others measure;
So there she waits, and while she lives,
And death forgets, and faith forgives,
Her memories go foraging
For bits of childhood song they treasure.

And like a giant harp that hums
On always, and is always blending
The coming of what never comes
With what has past and had an ending,
The City trembles, throbs, and pounds
Outside, and through a thousand sounds
The small intolerable drums
Of Time are like slow drops descending.

Bereft enough to shame a sage
And given little to long sighing,
With no illusion to assuage
The lonely changelessness of dying,—
Unsought, unthought-of, and unheard,
She sings and watches like a bird,
Safe in a comfortable cage
From which there will be no more flying.

Theophilus

By what serene malevolence of names
Had you the gift of yours, Theophilus?
Not even a smeared young Cyclops at his games
Would have you long,—and you are one of us.

Told of your deeds I shudder for your dreams
And they, no doubt, are few and innocent.
Meanwhile, I marvel; for in you, it seems,
Heredity outshines environment.

What lingering bit of Belial, unforeseen,
Survives and amplifies itself in you?
What manner of devilry has ever been
That your obliquity may never do?

Humility befits a father's eyes,
But not a friend of us would have him weep.
Admiring everything that lives and dies,
Theophilus, we like you best asleep.

Sleep—sleep; and let us find another man
To lend another name less hazardous:
Caligula, maybe, or Caliban,
Or Cain,—but surely not Theophilus.

Uncle Ananias

His words were magic and his heart was true,
  And everywhere he wandered he was blessed.
Out of all ancient men my childhood knew
  I choose him and I mark him for the best.
Of all authoritative liars, too,
  I crown him loveliest.

How fondly I remember the delight
  That always glorified him in the spring;
The joyous courage and the benedight
  Profusion of his faith in everything!
He was a good old man, and it was right
  That he should have his fling.

And often, underneath the apple-trees,
  When we surprised him in the summer time,
With what superb magnificence and ease
  He sinned enough to make the day sublime!
And if he liked us there about his knees,
  Truly it was no crime.

All summer long we loved him for the same
  Perennial inspiration of his lies;
And when the russet wealth of autumn came,
  There flew but fairer visions to our eyes—
Multiple, tropical, winged with a feathery flame,
  Like birds of paradise.

So to the sheltered end of many a year
  He charmed the seasons out with pageantry
Wearing upon his forehead, with no fear,
  The laurel of approved iniquity.
And every child who knew him, far or near,
  Did love him faithfully.

Bewick Finzer

TIME was when his half million drew
  The breath of six per cent;
But soon the worm of what-was-not
  Fed hard on his content;
And something crumbled in his brain
  When his half million went.

Time passed, and filled along with his
  The place of many more;
Time came, and hardly one of us
  Had credence to restore,
From what appeared one day, the man
  Whom we had known before.

The broken voice, the withered neck,
  The coat worn out with care,
The cleanliness of indigence,
  The brilliance of despair,
The fond imponderable dreams
  Of affluence,—all were there.

Poor Finzer, with his dreams and schemes,
  Fares hard now in the race,
With heart and eye that have a task
  When he looks in the face
Of one who might so easily
  Have been in Finzer's place.

He comes unfailing for the loan
  We give and then forget;
He comes, and probably for years
  Will he be coming yet,—
Familiar as an old mistake,
  And futile as regret.

Siege Perilous

Long warned of many terrors more severe
To scorch him than hell's engines could awaken,
He scanned again, too far to be so near,
The fearful seat no man had ever taken.

So many other men with older eyes
Than his to see with older sight behind them
Had known so long their one way to be wise,—
Was any other thing to do than mind them?

So many a blasting parallel had seared
Confusion on his faith,—could he but wonder
If he were mad and right, or if he feared
God's fury told in shafted flame and thunder?

There fell one day upon his eyes a light
Ethereal, and he heard no more men speaking;
He saw their shaken heads, but no long sight
Was his but for the end that he went seeking.

The end he sought was not the end; the crown
He won shall unto many still be given.
Moreover, there was reason here to frown:
No fury thundered, no flame fell from heaven.

The Voice of Age

SHE'D look upon us, if she could,
As hard as Rhadamanthus would;
Yet one may see,—who sees her face,
Her crown of silver and of lace,
Her mystical serene address
Of age alloyed with loveliness,—
That she would not annihilate
The frailest of things animate.

She has opinions of our ways,
And if we're not all mad, she says,—
If our ways are not wholly worse
Than others, for not being hers,—
There might somehow be found a few
Less insane things for us to do,
And we might have a little heed
Of what Belshazzar couldn't read.

She feels, with all our furniture,
Room yet for something more secure
Than our self-kindled aureoles
To guide our poor forgotten souls;
But when we have explained that grace
Dwells now in doing for the race,
She nods—as if she were relieved;
Almost as if she were deceived.

She frowns at much of what she hears,
And shakes her head, and has her fears;
Though none may know, by any chance,
What rose-leaf ashes of romance
Are faintly stirred by later days
That would be well enough, she says,
If only people were more wise,
And grown-up children used their eyes.

Richard Cory

WHENEVER Richard Cory went down town,
We people on the pavement looked at him:
He was a gentleman from sole to crown,
Clean favored, and imperially slim.

And he was always quietly arrayed,
And he was always human when he talked;
But still he fluttered pulses when he said,
"Good-morning," and he glittered when he walked.

And he was rich—yes, richer than a king—
And admirably schooled in every grace:
In fine, we thought that he was everything
To make us wish that we were in his place.

So on we worked, and waited for the light,
And went without the meat, and cursed the bread;
And Richard Cory, one calm summer night,
Went home and put a bullet through his head.

An Evangelist's Wife

"Why am I not myself these many days,
You ask? And have you nothing more to ask?
I do you wrong? I do not hear your praise
To God for giving you me to share your task?

"Jealous—of Her? Because her cheeks are pink,
And she has eyes? No, not if she had seven.
If you should only steal an hour to think,
Sometime, there might be less to be forgiven.

"No, you are never cruel. If once or twice
I found you so, I could applaud and sing.
Jealous of—What? You are not very wise.
Does not the good Book tell you anything?

"In David's time poor Michal had to go.
Jealous of God? Well, if you like it so."

Vickery's Mountain

BLUE in the west the mountain stands,
  And through the long twilight
Vickery sits with folded hands,
  And Vickery's eyes are bright.

Bright, for he knows what no man else
  On earth as yet may know:
There's a golden word that he never tells,
  And a gift that he will not show.

He dreams of honor and wealth and fame,
  He smiles, and well he may;
For to Vickery once a sick man came
  Who did not go away.

The day before the day to be,
  "Vickery," said the guest,
"You know as you live what's left of me—
  And you shall know the rest.

"You know as you live that I have come
  To this we call the end.
No doubt you have found me troublesome,
  But you've also found a friend;

"For we shall give and you shall take
  The gold that is in view;
The mountain there and I shall make
  A golden man of you.

"And you shall leave a friend behind
  Who neither frets nor feels;
And you shall move among your kind
  With hundreds at your heels.

"Now this that I have written here
    Tells all that need be told;
So, Vickery, take the way that's clear,
    And be a man of gold."

Vickery turned his eyes again
    To the far mountain-side,
And wept a tear for worthy men
    Defeated and defied.

Since then a crafty score of years
    Have come, and they have gone;
But Vickery counts no lost arrears:
    He lingers and lives on.

Blue in the west the mountain stands,
    Familiar as a face.
Blue, but Vickery knows what sands
    Are golden at its base.

He dreams and lives upon the day
    When he shall walk with kings.
Vickery smiles—and well he may.
    The life-caged linnet sings.

Vickery thinks the time will come
    To go for what is his;
But hovering, unseen hands at home
    Will hold him where he is.

There's a golden word that he never tells
    And a gift that he will not show.
All to be given to some one else—
    And Vickery not to know.

The Tree in Pamela's Garden

PAMELA was too gentle to deceive
Her roses. "Let the men stay where they are,"
She said, "and if Apollo's avatar
Be one of them, I shall not have to grieve."
And so she made all Tilbury Town believe
She sighed a little more for the North Star
Than over men, and only in so far
As she was in a garden was like Eve.

Her neighbors—doing all that neighbors can
To make romance of reticence meanwhile—
Seeing that she had never loved a man,
Wished Pamela had a cat, or a small bird,
And only would have wondered at her smile
Could they have seen that she had overheard.

II

PASSIONS

"With a gleam of heaven to make them pure,
And a glimmer of hell to make them human."
"HER EYES"

The Story of the Ashes
and the Flame

No matter why, nor whence, nor when she came,
There was her place. No matter what men said,
No matter what she was; living or dead,
Faithful or not, he loved her all the same.
The story was as old as human shame,
But ever since that lonely night she fled,
With books to blind him, he had only read
The story of the ashes and the flame.

There she was always coming pretty soon
To fool him back, with penitent scared eyes
That had in them the laughter of the moon
For baffled lovers, and to make him think—
Before she gave him time enough to wink—
Her kisses were the keys to Paradise.

Her Eyes

Up from the street and the crowds that went,
  Morning and midnight, to and fro,
Still was the room where his days he spent,
  And the stars were bleak, and the nights were slow.

Year after year, with his dream shut fast,
  He suffered and strove till his eyes were dim,
For the love that his brushes had earned at last,
  And the whole world rang with the praise of him.

But he cloaked his triumph, and searched, instead,
  Till his cheeks were sere and his hairs were gray.
"There are women enough, God knows," he said . . .
  "There are stars enough—when the sun's away."

Then he went back to the same still room
  That had held his dream in the long ago,
When he buried his days in a nameless tomb,
  And the stars were bleak, and the nights were slow.

And a passionate humor seized him there—
  Seized him and held him until there grew
Like life on his canvas, glowing and fair,
  A perilous face—and an angel's too.

Angel and maiden, and all in one,—
  All but the eyes. They were there, but yet
They seemed somehow like a soul half done.
  What was the matter? Did God forget? . . .

But he wrought them at last with a skill so sure
  That her eyes were the eyes of a deathless woman,—
With a gleam of heaven to make them pure,
  And a glimmer of hell to make them human.

God never forgets.—And he worships her
  There in that same still room of his,
For his wife, and his constant arbiter
  Of the world that was and the world that is.

And he wonders yet what her love could be
  To punish him after that strife so grim;
But the longer he lives with her eyes to see,
  The plainer it all comes back to him.

Reuben Bright

BECAUSE he was a butcher and thereby
Did earn an honest living (and did right),
I would not have you think that Reuben Bright
Was any more a brute than you or I;
For when they told him that his wife must die,
He stared at them, and shook with grief and fright,
And cried like a great baby half that night,
And made the women cry to see him cry.

And after she was dead, and he had paid
The singers and the sexton and the rest,
He packed a lot of things that she had made
Most mournfully away in an old chest
Of hers, and put some chopped-up cedar boughs
In with them, and tore down the slaughter-house.

Job the Rejected

THEY met, and overwhelming her distrust
With penitence, he praised away her fear;
They married, and Job gave him half a year
To wreck the temple, as we knew he must.
He fumbled hungrily to readjust
A fallen altar, but the road was clear
By which it was her will to disappear
That evening when Job found him in the dust.

Job would have deprecated such a way
Of heaving fuel on a sacred fire,
Yet even the while we saw it going out,
Hardly was Job to find his hour to shout;
And Job was not, so far as we could say,
The confirmation of her soul's desire.

Firelight

Ten years together without yet a cloud,
They seek each other's eyes at intervals
Of gratefulness to firelight and four walls
For love's obliteration of the crowd.
Serenely and perennially endowed
And bowered as few may be, their joy recalls
No snake, no sword; and over them there falls
The blessing of what neither says aloud.

Wiser for silence, they were not so glad
Were she to read the graven tale of lines
On the wan face of one somewhere alone;
Nor were they more content could he have had
Her thoughts a moment since of one who shines
Apart, and would be hers if he had known.

Ben Trovato

THE deacon thought. "I know them," he began,
"And they are all you ever heard of them—
Allurable to no sure theorem,
The scorn or the humility of man.
You say 'Can I believe it?'—and I can;
And I'm unwilling even to condemn
The benefaction of a stratagem
Like hers—and I'm a Presbyterian.

"Though blind, with but a wandering hour to live,
He felt the other woman in the fur
That now the wife had on. Could she forgive
All that? Apparently. Her rings were gone,
Of course; and when he found that she had none,
He smiled—as he had never smiled at her."

The Gift of God

BLESSED with a joy that only she
Of all alive shall ever know,
She wears a proud humility
For what it was that willed it so,—
That her degree should be so great
Among the favored of the Lord
That she may scarcely bear the weight
Of her bewildering reward.

As one apart, immune, alone,
Or featured for the shining ones,
And like to none that she has known
Of other women's other sons,—
The firm fruition of her need,
He shines anointed; and he blurs
Her vision, till it seems indeed
A sacrilege to call him hers.

She fears a little for so much
Of what is best, and hardly dares
To think of him as one to touch
With aches, indignities, and cares;
She sees him rather at the goal,
Still shining; and her dream foretells
The proper shining of a soul
Where nothing ordinary dwells.

Perchance a canvass of the town
Would find him far from flags and shouts,
And leave him only the renown
Of many smiles and many doubts;
Perchance the crude and common tongue
Would havoc strangely with his worth;
But she, with innocence unwrung,
Would read his name around the earth.

And others, knowing how this youth
Would shine, if love could make him great,
When caught and tortured for the truth
Would only writhe and hesitate;
While she, arranging for his days
What centuries could not fulfill,
Transmutes him with her faith and praise,
And has him shining where she will.

She crowns him with her gratefulness,
And says again that life is good;
And should the gift of God be less
In him than in her motherhood,
His fame, though vague, will not be small,
As upward through her dream he fares,
Half clouded with a crimson fall
Of roses thrown on marble stairs.

Vain Gratuities

Never was there a man much uglier
In eyes of other women, or more grim:
"The Lord has filled her chalice to the brim,
So let us pray she's a philosopher,"
They said; and there was more they said of her—
Deeming it, after twenty years with him,
No wonder that she kept her figure slim
And always made you think of lavender.

But she, demure as ever, and as fair,
Almost, as they remembered her before
She found him, would have laughed had she been there;
And all they said would have been heard no more
Than foam that washes on an island shore
Where there are none to listen or to care.

The Companion

LET him answer as he will,
Or be lightsome as he may,
Now nor after shall he say
Worn-out words enough to kill,
Or to lull down by their craft,
Doubt, that was born yesterday,
When he lied and when she laughed.

Let him find another name
For the starlight on the snow,
Let him teach her till she know
That all seasons are the same,
And all sheltered ways are fair,—
Still, wherever she may go,
Doubt will have a dwelling there.

The Clinging Vine

"BE calm? And was I frantic?
   You'll have me laughing soon.
I'm calm as this Atlantic,
   And quiet as the moon;
I may have spoken faster
   Than once, in other days;
For I've no more a master,
   And now—'Be calm,' he says.

"Fear not, fear no commotion,—
   I'll be as rocks and sand;
The moon and stars and ocean
   Will envy my command;
No creature could be stiller
   In any kind of place
Than I . . . No, I'll not kill her;
   Her death is in her face.

"Be happy while she has it,
   For she'll not have it long;
A year, and then you'll pass it,
   Preparing a new song.
And I'm a fool for prating
   Of what a year may bring,
When more like her are waiting
   For more like you to sing.

"You mock me with denial,
   You mean to call me hard?
You see no room for trial
   When all my doors are barred?
You say, and you'd say dying,
   That I dream what I know;
And sighing, and denying,
   You'd hold my hand and go.

"You scowl—and I don't wonder;
    I spoke too fast again;
But you'll forgive one blunder,
    For you are like most men:
You are,—or so you've told me,
    So many mortal times,
That heaven ought not to hold me
    Accountable for crimes.

"Be calm? Was I unpleasant?
    Then I'll be more discreet,
And grant you, for the present,
    The balm of my defeat:
What she, with all her striving,
    Could not have brought about,
You've done. Your own contriving
    Has put the last light out.

"If she were the whole story,
    If worse were not behind,
I'd creep with you to glory,
    Believing I was blind;
I'd creep, and go on seeming
    To be what I despise.
You laugh, and say I'm dreaming,
    And all your laughs are lies.

"Are women mad? A few are,
    And if it's true you say—
If most men are as you are—
    We'll all be mad some day.
Be calm—and let me finish;
    There's more for you to know.
I'll talk while you diminish,
    And listen while you grow.

"There was a man who married
  Because he couldn't see;
And all his days he carried
  The mark of his degree.
But you—you came clear-sighted,
  And found truth in my eyes;
And all my wrongs you've righted
  With lies, and lies, and lies.

"You've killed the last assurance
  That once would have me strive
To rouse an old endurance
  That is no more alive.
It makes two people chilly
  To say what we have said,
But you—you'll not be silly
  And wrangle for the dead.

"You don't? You never wrangle?
  Why scold then,—or complain?
More words will only mangle
  What you've already slain.
Your pride you can't surrender?
  My name—for that you fear?
Since when were men so tender,
  And honor so severe?

"No more—I'll never bear it.
  I'm going. I'm like ice.
My burden? You would share it?
  Forbid the sacrifice!
Forget so quaint a notion,
  And let no more be told;
For moon and stars and ocean
  And you and I are cold."

The Growth of "Lorraine"

I

WHILE I stood listening, discreetly dumb,
Lorraine was having the last word with me:
"I know," she said, "I know it, but you see
Some creatures are born fortunate, and some
Are born to be found out and overcome,—
Born to be slaves, to let the rest go free;
And if I'm one of them (and I must be)
You may as well forget me and go home.

"You tell me not to say these things, I know,
But I should never try to be content:
I've gone too far; the life would be too slow.
Some could have done it—some girls have the stuff;
But I can't do it: I don't know enough.
I'm going to the devil."—And she went.

II

I DID not half believe her when she said
That I should never hear from her again;
Nor when I found a letter from Lorraine,
Was I surprised or grieved at what I read:
"Dear friend, when you find this, I shall be dead.
You are too far away to make me stop.
They say that one drop—think of it, one drop!—
Will be enough,—but I'll take five instead.

"You do not frown because I call you friend,
For I would have you glad that I still keep
Your memory, and even at the end—
Impenitent, sick, shattered—cannot curse
The love that flings, for better or for worse,
This worn-out, cast-out flesh of mine to sleep."

59

Llewellyn and the Tree

COULD he have made Priscilla share
    The paradise that he had planned,
Llewellyn would have loved his wife
    As well as any in the land.

Could he have made Priscilla cease
    To goad him for what God left out,
Llewellyn would have been as mild
    As any we have read about.

Could all have been as all was not,
    Llewellyn would have had no story;
He would have stayed a quiet man
    And gone his quiet way to glory.

But howsoever mild he was
    Priscilla was implacable;
And whatsoever timid hopes
    He built—she found them, and they fell.

And this went on, with intervals
    Of labored harmony between
Resounding discords, till at last
    Llewellyn turned—as will be seen.

Priscilla, warmer than her name,
    And shriller than the sound of saws,
Pursued Llewellyn once too far,
    Not knowing quite the man he was.

The more she said, the fiercer clung
    The stinging garment of his wrath;
And this was all before the day
    When Time tossed roses in his path.

Before the roses ever came
 Llewellyn had already risen.
The roses may have ruined him,
 They may have kept him out of prison.

And she who brought them, being Fate,
 Made roses do the work of spears,—
Though many made no more of her
 Than civet, coral, rouge, and years.

You ask us what Llewellyn saw,
 But why ask what may not be given?
To some will come a time when change
 Itself is beauty, if not heaven.

One afternoon Priscilla spoke,
 And her shrill history was done;
At any rate, she never spoke
 Like that again to anyone.

One gold October afternoon
 Great fury smote the silent air;
And then Llewellyn leapt and fled
 Like one with hornets in his hair.

Llewellyn left us, and he said
 Forever, leaving few to doubt him;
And so, through frost and clicking leaves,
 The Tilbury way went on without him.

And slowly, through the Tilbury mist,
 The stillness of October gold
Went out like beauty from a face.
 Priscilla watched it, and grew old.

He fled, still clutching in his flight
   The roses that had been his fall;
The Scarlet One, as you surmise,
   Fled with him, coral, rouge, and all.

Priscilla, waiting, saw the change
   Of twenty slow October moons;
And then she vanished, in her turn
   To be forgotten, like old tunes.

So they were gone—all three of them,
   I should have said, and said no more,
Had not a face once on Broadway
   Been one that I had seen before.

The face and hands and hair were old,
   But neither time nor penury
Could quench within Llewellyn's eyes
   The shine of his one victory.

The roses, faded and gone by,
   Left ruin where they once had reigned;
But on the wreck, as on old shells,
   The color of the rose remained.

His fictive merchandise I bought
   For him to keep and show again,
Then led him slowly from the crush
   Of his cold-shouldered fellow men.

"And so, Llewellyn," I began—
   "Not so," he said; "not so at all:
I've tried the world, and found it good,
   For more than twenty years this fall.

"And what the world has left of me
  Will go now in a little while."
And what the world had left of him
  Was partly an unholy guile.

"That I have paid for being calm
  Is what you see, if you have eyes;
For let a man be calm too long,
  He pays for much before he dies.

"Be calm when you are growing old
  And you have nothing else to do;
Pour not the wine of life too thin
  If water means the death of you.

"You say I might have learned at home
  The truth in season to be strong?
Not so; I took the wine of life
  Too thin, and I was calm too long.

"Like others who are strong too late,
  For me there was no going back;
For I had found another speed,
  And I was on the other track.

"God knows how far I might have gone
  Or what there might have been to see;
But my speed had a sudden end,
  And here you have the end of me."

The end or not, it may be now
  But little farther from the truth
To say those worn satiric eyes
  Had something of immortal youth.

He may among the millions here
　　Be one; or he may, quite as well,
Be gone to find again the Tree
　　Of Knowledge, out of which he fell.

He may be near us, dreaming yet
　　Of unrepented rouge and coral;
Or in a grave without a name
　　May be as far off as a moral.

Another Dark Lady

THINK not, because I wonder where you fled,
That I would lift a pin to see you there;
• You may, for me, be prowling anywhere,
So long as you show not your little head:
No dark and evil story of the dead
Would leave you less pernicious or less fair—
Not even Lilith, with her famous hair;
And Lilith was the devil, I have read.

I cannot hate you, for I loved you then.
The woods were golden then. There was a road
Through beeches; and I said their smooth feet showed
Like yours. Truth must have heard me from afar;
For I shall never have to learn again
That yours are cloven as no beech's are.

The Unforgiven

WHEN he, who is the unforgiven,
Beheld her first, he found her fair:
No promise ever dreamt in heaven
Could then have lured him anywhere
That would have been away from there;
And all his wits had lightly striven,
Foiled with her voice, and eyes, and hair.

There's nothing in the saints and sages
To meet the shafts her glances had,
Or such as hers have had for ages
To blind a man till he be glad,
And humble him till he be mad.
The story would have many pages,
And would be neither good nor bad.

And, having followed, you would find him
Where properly the play begins;
But look for no red light behind him—
No fumes of many-colored sins,
Fanned high by screaming violins.
God knows what good it was to blind him,
Or whether man or woman wins.

And by the same eternal token,
Who knows just how it will all end?—
This drama of hard words unspoken,
This fireside farce, without a friend
Or enemy to comprehend
What augurs when two lives are broken,
And fear finds nothing left to mend.

He stares in vain for what awaits him,
And sees in Love a coin to toss;
He smiles, and her cold hush berates him
Beneath his hard half of the cross;
They wonder why it ever was;
And she, the unforgiving, hates him
More for her lack than for her loss.

He feeds with pride his indecision,
And shrinks from what will not occur,
Bequeathing with infirm derision
His ashes to the days that were,
Before she made him prisoner;
And labors to retrieve the vision
That he must once have had of her.

He waits, and there awaits an ending,
And he knows neither what nor when;
But no magicians are attending
To make him see as he saw then,
And he will never find again
The face that once had been the rending
Of all his purpose among men.

He blames her not, nor does he chide her,
And she has nothing new to say;
If he were Bluebeard he could hide her,
But that's not written in the play,
And there will be no change to-day;
Although, to the serene outsider,
There still would seem to be a way.

Eros Turannos

SHE fears him, and will always ask
  What fated her to choose him;
She meets in his engaging mask
  All reasons to refuse him;
But what she meets and what she fears
Are less than are the downward years,
Drawn slowly to the foamless weirs
  Of age, were she to lose him.

Between a blurred sagacity
  That once had power to sound him,
And Love, that will not let him be
  The Judas that she found him,
Her pride assuages her almost,
As if it were alone the cost.—
He sees that he will not be lost,
  And waits and looks around him.

A sense of ocean and old trees
  Envelops and allures him;
Tradition, touching all he sees,
  Beguiles and reassures him;
And all her doubts of what he says
Are dimmed with what she knows of days—
Till even prejudice delays
  And fades, and she secures him.

The falling leaf inaugurates
  The reign of her confusion;
The pounding wave reverberates
  The dirge of her illusion;
And home, where passion lived and died,
Becomes a place where she can hide,
While all the town and harbor side
  Vibrate with her seclusion.

We tell you, tapping on our brows,
    The story as it should be,—
As if the story of a house
    Were told, or ever could be;
We'll have no kindly veil between
Her visions and those we have seen,—
As if we guessed what hers have been,
    Or what they are or would be.

Meanwhile we do no harm; for they
    That with a god have striven,
Not hearing much of what we say,
    Take what the god has given;
Though like waves breaking it may be,
Or like a changed familiar tree,
Or like a stairway to the sea
    Where down the blind are driven.

Luke Havergal

Go to the western gate, Luke Havergal,
There where the vines cling crimson on the wall,
And in the twilight wait for what will come.
The leaves will whisper there of her, and some,
Like flying words, will strike you as they fall;
But go, and if you listen she will call.
Go to the western gate, Luke Havergal—
Luke Havergal.

No, there is not a dawn in eastern skies
To rift the fiery night that's in your eyes;
But there, where western glooms are gathering,
The dark will end the dark, if anything:
God slays Himself with every leaf that flies,
And hell is more than half of paradise.
No, there is not a dawn in eastern skies—
In eastern skies.

Out of a grave I come to tell you this,
Out of a grave I come to quench the kiss
That flames upon your forehead with a glow
That binds you to the way that you must go.
Yes, there is yet one way to where she is,
Bitter, but one that faith may never miss.
Out of a grave I come to tell you this—
To tell you this.

There is the western gate, Luke Havergal,
There are the crimson leaves upon the wall.
Go, for the winds are tearing them away,—
Nor think to riddle the dead words they say,
Nor any more to feel them as they fall;
But go, and if you trust her she will call.
There is the western gate, Luke Havergal—
Luke Havergal.

III

THE DEAD

> "... and thus we die,
> Still searching, like poor old astronomers
> Who totter off to bed and go to sleep,
> To dream of untriangulated stars."
>
> "OCTAVES"

A Man in Our Town

We pitied him as one too much at ease
With Nemesis and impending indigence;
Also, as if by way of recompense,
We sought him always in extremities;
And while ways more like ours had more to please
Our common code than his improvidence,
There lurked alive in our experience
His homely genius for emergencies.

He was not one for men to marvel at,
And yet there was another neighborhood
When he was gone, and many a thrifty tear.
There was an increase in a man like that;
And though he be forgotten, it was good
For more than one of you that he was here.

Exit

FOR what we owe to other days,
Before we poisoned him with praise,
May we who shrank to find him weak
Remember that he cannot speak.

For envy that we may recall,
And for our faith before the fall,
May we who are alive be slow
To tell what we shall never know.

For penance he would not confess,
And for the fateful emptiness
Of early triumph undermined,
May we now venture to be kind.

Amaryllis

ONCE, when I wandered in the woods alone,
An old man tottered up to me and said,
"Come, friend, and see the grave that I have made
For Amaryllis." There was in the tone
Of his complaint such quaver and such moan
That I took pity on him and obeyed,
And long stood looking where his hands had laid
An ancient woman, shrunk to skin and bone.

Far out beyond the forest I could hear
The calling of loud progress, and the bold
Incessant scream of commerce ringing clear;
But though the trumpets of the world were glad,
It made me lonely and it made me sad
To think that Amaryllis had grown old.

Charles Carville's Eyes

A MELANCHOLY face Charles Carville had,
But not so melancholy as it seemed,
When once you knew him, for his mouth redeemed
His insufficient eyes, forever sad:
In them there was no life-glimpse, good or bad,
Nor joy nor passion in them ever gleamed;
His mouth was all of him that ever beamed,
His eyes were sorry, but his mouth was glad.

He never was a fellow that said much,
And half of what he did say was not heard
By many of us: we were out of touch
With all his whims and all his theories
Till he was dead, so those blank eyes of his
Might speak them. Then we heard them, every word.

Souvenir

A VANISHED house that for an hour I knew
By some forgotten chance when I was young
Had once a glimmering window overhung
With honeysuckle wet with evening dew.
Along the path tall dusky dahlias grew,
And shadowy hydrangeas reached and swung
Ferociously; and over me, among
The moths and mysteries, a blurred bat flew.

Somewhere within there were dim presences
Of days that hovered and of years gone by.
I waited, and between their silences
There was an evanescent faded noise;
And though a child, I knew it was the voice
Of one whose occupation was to die.

Hector Kane

If Hector Kane at eighty-five
Was not the youngest man alive,
Appearance had anointed him
  With undiminished youth.
To look at him was to believe
That as we ask we may receive,
Annoyed by no such evil whim
  As death, or time, or truth.

Which is to doubt, if any of you,
Seeing him, had believed him true.
He was too young to be so old,
  Too old to be so fair.
Beneath a snowy crown of curls,
His cheeks that might have been a girl's
Were certainly, if truth were told,
  Too rose-like to be there.

But Hector was a child of earth,
And would have held of little worth
Reflection or misgiving cast
  On his reality.
It was a melancholy crime,
No less, to torture life with time;
And whoso did was first and last
  Creation's enemy.

He told us, one convivial night,
When younger men were not so bright
Or brisk as he, how he had spared
  His heart a world of pain,
Merely by seeing always clear
What most it was he wanted here,
And having it when most he cared,
  And having it again.

"You children of threescore or so,"
He said, "had best begin to know
If your infirmities that ache,
    Your lethargies and fears,
And doubts, are mostly more or less
Like things a drunkard in distress
May count with horror, while you shake
    For counting days and years.

"Nothing was ever true for me
Until I found it so," said he;
"So time for me has always been
    Four letters of a word.
Time? Is it anything to eat?
Or maybe it has legs and feet,
To go so as to be unseen;
    Or maybe it's a bird.

"Years? I have never seen such things.
Why let your fancy give them wings
To lift you from experience
    And carry you astray?
If only you will not be old,
Your mines will give you more than gold,
And for a cheerful diligence
    Will keep the worm away.

"We die of what we eat and drink,
But more we die of what we think;
For which you see me still as young
    At heart as heretofore.
So here's to what's awaiting us—
Cras ingens iterabimus—"
A clutch of wonder gripped his tongue,
    And Hector said no more.

Serene and inarticulate
He lay, for us to contemplate.
The mortal trick, we all agreed,
   Was never better turned:
Bequeathing us to time and care,
He told us yet that we were there
To make as much as we could read
   Of all that he had learned.

For a Dead Lady

No more with overflowing light
Shall fill the eyes that now are faded,
Nor shall another's fringe with night
Their woman-hidden world as they did.
No more shall quiver down the days
The flowing wonder of her ways,
Whereof no language may requite
The shifting and the many-shaded.

The grace, divine, definitive,
Clings only as a faint forestalling;
The laugh that love could not forgive
Is hushed, and answers to no calling;
The forehead and the little ears
Have gone where Saturn keeps the years;
The breast where roses could not live
Has done with rising and with falling.

The beauty, shattered by the laws
That have creation in their keeping,
No longer trembles at applause,
Or over children that are sleeping;
And we who delve in beauty's lore
Know all that we have known before
Of what inexorable cause
Makes Time so vicious in his reaping.

The Whip

THE doubt you fought so long,
The cynic net you cast,
The tyranny, the wrong,
The ruin, they are past;
And here you are at last,
Your blood no longer vexed.
The coffin has you fast,
The clod will have you next.

But fear you not the clod,
Nor ever doubt the grave:
The roses and the sod
Will not forswear the wave.
The gift the river gave
Is now but theirs to cover:
The mistress and the slave
Are gone now, and the lover.

You left the two to find
Their own way to the brink
Then—shall I call you blind?—
You chose to plunge and sink.
God knows the gall we drink
Is not the mead we cry for,
Nor was it, I should think—
For you—a thing to die for.

Could we have done the same,
Had we been in your place?—
This funeral of your name
Throws no light on the case.
Could we have made the chase,
And felt then as you felt?—
But what's this on your face,
Blue, curious, like a welt?

There were some ropes of sand
Recorded long ago,
But none, I understand,
Of water. Is it so?
And she—she struck the blow,
You but a neck behind. . .
You saw the river flow—
Still, shall I call you blind?

The Mill

THE miller's wife had waited long,
    The tea was cold, the fire was dead;
And there might yet be nothing wrong
    In how he went and what he said:
"There are no millers any more,"
    Was all that she had heard him say;
And he had lingered at the door
    So long that it seemed yesterday.

Sick with a fear that had no form
    She knew that she was there at last;
And in the mill there was a warm
    And mealy fragrance of the past.
What else there was would only seem
    To say again what he had meant;
And what was hanging from a beam
    Would not have heeded where she went.

And if she thought it followed her,
    She may have reasoned in the dark
That one way of the few there were
    Would hide her and would leave no mark:
Black water, smooth above the weir
    Like starry velvet in the night,
Though ruffled once, would soon appear
    The same as ever to the sight.

The Rat

As often as he let himself be seen
We pitied him, or scorned him, or deplored
The inscrutable profusion of the Lord
Who shaped as one of us a thing so mean—
Who made him human when he might have been
A rat, and so been wholly in accord
With any other creature we abhorred
As always useless and not always clean.

Now he is hiding all alone somewhere,
And in a final hole not ready then;
For now he is among those over there
Who are not coming back to us again.
And we who do the fiction of our share
Say less of rats and rather more of men.

Inferential

ALTHOUGH I saw before me there the face
Of one whom I had honored among men
The least, and on regarding him again
Would not have had him in another place,
He fitted with an unfamiliar grace
The coffin where I could not see him then
As I had seen him and appraised him when
I deemed him unessential to the race.

For there was more of him than what I saw.
And there was on me more than the old awe
That is the common genius of the dead.
I might as well have heard him: "Never mind;
If some of us were not so far behind,
The rest of us were not so far ahead."

Leonora

THEY have made for Leonora this low dwelling in the ground,
And with cedar they have woven the four walls round.
Like a little dryad hiding she'll be wrapped all in green,
Better kept and longer valued than by ways that would have been.

They will come with many roses in the early afternoon,
They will come with pinks and lilies and with Leonora soon;
And as long as beauty's garments over beauty's limbs are thrown,
There'll be lilies that are liars, and the rose will have its own.

There will be a wondrous quiet in the house that they have made,
And tonight will be a darkness in the place where she'll be laid;
But the builders, looking forward into time, could only see
Darker nights for Leonora than tonight shall ever be.

How Annandale Went Out

"THEY called it Annandale—and I was there
To flourish, to find words, and to attend:
Liar, physician, hypocrite, and friend,
I watched him; and the sight was not so fair
As one or two that I have seen elsewhere:
An apparatus not for me to mend—
A wreck, with hell between him and the end,
Remained of Annandale; and I was there.

"I knew the ruin as I knew the man;
So put the two together, if you can,
Remembering the worst you know of me.
Now view yourself as I was, on the spot—
With a slight kind of engine. Do you see?
Like this . . . You wouldn't hang me? I thought not."

Annandale Again

ALMOST as if my thought of him
Had called him from he said not where,
He knocked. I knew him through the door,
And Annandale was waiting there.

Nothing of years or distances,
Or deserts that he may have ranged,
Betrayed him. He was Annandale,
The only man who never changed.

"Do as you must," he said, "and God
Will say that you have done no wrong.
Begin by disappointing me,
And ask where I have been so long.

"What matter's it where I have been,
Or on what mountain or what star?
All places are as much alike
As all men and all women are—

"Which is not much. The best of us
Are curiously unlike the worst;
And for some time, at any rate,
The last shall never be the first.

"Wherefore I leave them, having done
No harm to them, or none to show."—
There was no liking such a man;
You loved him, or you let him go.

"Dreamers who crave a common yoke
For bulls and ewes and elephants
May have it; and my having mine
May be a soothing circumstance

"For you and me, and for my wife;
I mean my new wife Damaris.
I'll tell you, if you must be told,
The sort of woman that she is.

"When Miriam died, my former wife,
I wept and said that all was done;
Yet even as long ago as then
My darkness had a smothered sun

"Behind it, trying to shine through.
More like a living voice of light
It was, than like the sun itself,
And my night was not wholly night.

"And my world was not wholly gone,
As I had feared. Well, hardly so.
I wonder we should learn to live,
Where there's so much for us to know.

"For that, we don't. We live meanwhile;
And then, with nothing learned, we die.
God has been very good to him
Whose end is not an asking why.

"But I'm astray, beginning ill
To lose myself in setting out;
It was my new wife Damaris
That you were asking me about.

"Your interest was an innocence,
And your concern was no surprise.
Well, I have brought her home with me,
And you may find her in my eyes.

"In general, there's no more to tell;
Yet there's this in particular:
She knows the way the good God made
My fur to lie; and there you are.

"And that's enough; you know the rest.
You know as much as I may learn,
Should we go to the end of time
Together, and through time return

"To now again. I should like that,
Ad infinitum. So you see
How graciously has fate prepared
A most agreeable trap for me.

"For where we stay because we must,
Prison or cage or sacrament,
We're in a trap. This world is one,
Obscurely sprung for our ascent,

"Maybe, till we are out of it,
And in another. Once I thought
My cage was dark; but there was light
To let me see that I was caught

"For always there, with Damaris
In the same cage. It's large enough
To hold as many as two of us,
With no constraint worth speaking of.

"The Keeper, who's invisible,
Reveals himself in many a sign,
To caution me that I shall read
And heed the benefits that are mine—

"I don't say hers. Still, if she likes
Her cage with me, and says it's home,
And sings in it, what shall I say
That you may not find wearisome?

"You doctors, who have found so much
In matter that it's hardly there,
May all, in your discomfiture,
Anon be on your knees in prayer

"For larger presence of what is
In what is not. Then you will see
Why Damaris, who knows everything,
Knows how to find so much in me.

"She finds what I have never found
Before; and there's a fearsome doubt,
Sometimes, that slumbers and awaits
A day when Damaris finds out

"How much of undistinguished man
There is in her new destiny.
When she divines it, I shall not
Be told, or not immediately—

"Nor ever, if I'm as amiable
As her attention apprehends.
I'm watching her, and hiding tight
Within me several odds and ends

"Of insights and forbearances
And cautious ways of being kind,
That she has dropped like handkerchiefs,
Conceivably for me to find.

"But one shall not acquire all this
At once, or so it would appear.
I've lain awake establishing
Her permutations in a year—

"Not always indispensable,
You say; and yet, for recompense,
Revealing, when it looks like rain,
A refuge of intelligence;

"Which, with all honor to the rest
That makes a cage enjoyable,
Is not the least of ornaments
That every woman may as well

"Inherit as an amulet
For disillusions unforeseen—
Assuming always that for her
May still be some that have not been.

"Meanwhile, perfection has a price
That humor always has to pay
With patience, as a man may learn
Of woman when she has her way.

"While Miriam lived, I made a book
To make another woman wise.
Blessed are they who are not born
Above instruction by surprise.

"But there was wisdom in it too;
And there are times her eyes are wet
With wonder that I should foresee
So much of her before we met.

"Again, when her complexities
Are restive, or she may have bruised
An elbow on the bars of home,
I may be for a time confused;

"But not for long. She gratifies
A casual need of giving pain;
And having drawn a little blood,
She folds her paws and purrs again.

"So all goes well; and with our wits
Awake, should go indefinitely—
Sufficient without subterfuge,
Harmonious without history.

"You'll find us cheerful prisoners
Enough, with nothing to bewail.
I've told you about Damaris;
And I'll go home."—Poor Annandale!

Poor Damaris! He did not go
So far as home that afternoon.
It may be they offended fate
With harmonies too much in tune

For a discordant earth to share
Unslain, or it may just have been,
Like stars and leaves and marmosets,
Fruition of a force unseen.

There was a sick crash in the street,
And after that there was no doubt
Of what there was; and I was there
To watch while Annandale went out.

No pleasure was awaiting me,
And there would have been none for you;
And mine was the one light I had
To show me the one thing to do.

Sometimes I'll ask myself, alone,
The measure of her debt to me
If some of him were still alive,
And motionless, for her to see;

Sometimes I'll ask if Annandale,
Could he have seen so far ahead,
Had been so sure as I am now
Of more than all he might have said.

I'll ask, and ask, and always ask,
And have no answer; or none yet.
The gain that lives in woman's loss
Is one that woman may forget

For a long time. A doctor knows
The nature of an accident;
And Damaris, who knows everything,
May still be asking what it meant.

Supremacy

THERE is a drear and lonely tract of hell
From all the common gloom removed afar:
A flat, sad land it is, where shadows are,
Whose lorn estate my verse may never tell.
I walked among them and I knew them well:
Men I had slandered on life's little star
For churls and sluggards; and I knew the scar
Upon their brows of woe ineffable.

But as I went majestic on my way,
Into the dark they vanished, one by one,
Till, with a shaft of God's eternal day,
The dream of all my glory was undone,—
And, with a fool's importunate dismay,
I heard the dead men singing in the sun.

IV

EDGE OF TOWN

"Like nothing that was ever bought or sold
It waited there, the body and the mind;
And with a mighty meaning of a kind
That tells the more the more it is not told."
"THE SHEAVES"

John Evereldown

"WHERE are you going to-night, to-night,—
  Where are you going, John Evereldown?
There's never the sign of a star in sight,
  Nor a lamp that's nearer than Tilbury Town.
Why do you stare as a dead man might?
Where are you pointing away from the light?
And where are you going to-night, to-night,—
  Where are you going, John Evereldown?"

"Right through the forest, where none can see,
  There's where I'm going, to Tilbury Town.
The men are asleep,—or awake, may be,—
  But the women are calling John Evereldown.
Ever and ever they call for me.
And while they call can a man be free?
So right through the forest, where none can see,
  There's where I'm going, to Tilbury Town."

"But why are you going so late, so late,—
  Why are you going, John Evereldown?
Though the road be smooth and the way be straight,
  There are two long leagues to Tilbury Town.
Come in by the fire, old man, and wait!
Why do you chatter out there by the gate?
And why are you going so late, so late,—
  Why are you going, John Evereldown?"

"I follow the women wherever they call,—
  That's why I'm going to Tilbury Town.
God knows if I pray to be done with it all,
  But God is no friend to John Evereldown.
So the clouds may come and the rain may fall,
The shadows may creep and the dead men crawl,—
But I follow the women wherever they call,
  And that's why I'm going to Tilbury Town."

The Tavern

WHENEVER I go by there nowadays
And look at the rank weeds and the strange grass,
The torn blue curtains and the broken glass,
I seem to be afraid of the old place;
And something stiffens up and down my face,
For all the world as if I saw the ghost
Of old Ham Amory, the murdered host,
With his dead eyes turned on me all aglaze.

The Tavern has a story, but no man
Can tell us what it is. We only know
That once long after midnight, years ago
A stranger galloped up from Tilbury Town,
Who brushed, and scared, and all but overran
That skirt-crazed reprobate, John Evereldown.

The House on the Hill

THEY are all gone away,
  The House is shut and still,
There is nothing more to say.

Through broken walls and gray
  The winds blow bleak and shrill:
They are all gone away.

Nor is there one to-day
  To speak them good or ill:
There is nothing more to say.

Why is it then we stray
  Around the sunken sill?
They are all gone away,

And our poor fancy-play
  For them is wasted skill:
There is nothing more to say.

There is ruin and decay
  In the House on the Hill:
They are all gone away,
There is nothing more to say.

Mr. Flood's Party

OLD Eben Flood, climbing alone one night
Over the hill between the town below
And the forsaken upland hermitage
That held as much as he should ever know
On earth again of home, paused warily.
The road was his with not a native near;
And Eben, having leisure, said aloud,
For no man else in Tillbury Town to hear:

"Well, Mr. Flood, we have the harvest moon
Again, and we may not have many more;
The bird is on the wing, the poet says,
And you and I have said it here before.
Drink to the bird." He raised up to the light
The jug that he had gone so far to fill,
And answered huskily: "Well, Mr. Flood,
Since you propose it, I believe I will."

Alone, as if enduring to the end
A valiant armor of scarred hopes outworn,
He stood there in the middle of the road
Like Roland's ghost winding a silent horn.
Below him, in the town among the trees,
Where friends of other days had honored him,
A phantom salutation of the dead
Rang thinly till old Eben's eyes were dim.

Then, as a mother lays her sleeping child
Down tenderly, fearing it may awake,
He set the jug down slowly at his feet
With trembling care, knowing that most things break;
And only when assured that on firm earth
It stood, as the uncertain lives of men
Assuredly did not, he paced away,
And with his hand extended paused again:

"Well, Mr. Flood, we have not met like this
In a long time; and many a change has come
To both of us, I fear, since last it was
We had a drop together. Welcome home!"
Convivially returning with himself,
Again he raised the jug up to the light;
And with an acquiescent quaver said:
"Well, Mr. Flood, if you insist, I might.

"Only a very little, Mr. Flood—
For auld lang syne. No more, sir; that will do."
So, for the time, apparently it did,
And Eben evidently thought so too;
For soon amid the silver loneliness
Of night he lifted up his voice and sang,
Secure, with only two moons listening,
Until the whole harmonious landscape rang—

"For auld lang syne." The weary throat gave out,
The last word wavered, and the song was done.
He raised again the jug regretfully
And shook his head, and was again alone.
There was not much that was ahead of him,
And there was nothing in the town below—
Where strangers would have shut the many doors
That many friends had opened long ago.

Isaac and Archibald

Isaac and Archibald were two old men.
I knew them, and I may have laughed at them
A little; but I must have honored them
For they were old, and they were good to me.

I do not think of either of them now,
Without remembering, infallibly,
A journey that I made one afternoon
With Isaac to find out what Archibald
Was doing with his oats. It was high time
Those oats were cut, said Isaac; and he feared
That Archibald—well, he could never feel
Quite sure of Archibald. Accordingly
The good old man invited me—that is,
Permitted me—to go along with him;
And I, with a small boy's adhesiveness
To competent old age, got up and went.
I do not know that I cared overmuch
For Archibald's or anybody's oats,
But Archibald was quite another thing,
And Isaac yet another; and the world
Was wide, and there was gladness everywhere.
We walked together down the River Road
With all the warmth and wonder of the land
Around us, and the wayside flash of leaves,—
And Isaac said the day was glorious;
But somewhere at the end of the first mile
I found that I was figuring to find
How long those ancient legs of his would keep
The pace that he had set for them. The sun
Was hot, and I was ready to sweat blood;
But Isaac, for aught I could make of him,
Was cool to his hat-band. So I said then
With a dry gasp of affable despair,
Something about the scorching days we have

In August without knowing it sometimes;
But Isaac said the day was like a dream,
And praised the Lord, and talked about the breeze.
I made a fair confession of the breeze,
And crowded casually on his thought
The nearness of a profitable nook
That I could see. First I was half inclined
To caution him that he was growing old,
But something that was not compassion soon
Made plain the folly of all subterfuge.
Isaac was old, but not so old as that.

So I proposed, without an overture,
That we be seated in the shade a while,
And Isaac made no murmur. Soon the talk
Was turned on Archibald, and I began
To feel some premonitions of a kind
That only childhood knows; for the old man
Had looked at me and clutched me with his eye,
And asked if I had ever noticed things.
I told him that I could not think of them,
And I knew then, by the frown that left his face
Unsatisfied, that I had injured him.
"My good young friend," he said, "you cannot feel
What I have seen so long. You have the eyes—
Oh, yes—but you have not the other things:
The sight within that never will deceive,
You do not know—you have no right to know;
The twilight warning of experience,
The singular idea of loneliness,—
These are not yours. But they have long been mine,
And they have shown me now for seven years
That Archibald is changing. It is not
So much that he should come to his last hand,
And leave the game, and go the old way down;
But I have known him in and out so long,
And I have seen so much of good in him

That other men have shared and have not seen,
And I have gone so far through thick and thin,
Through cold and fire with him, that now it brings
To this old heart of mine an ache that you
Have not yet lived enough to know about.
But even unto you, and your boy's faith,
Your freedom, and your untried confidence,
A time will come to find out what it means
To know that you are losing what was yours,
To know that you are being left behind;
And then the long contempt of innocence—
God bless you, boy!—don't think the worse of it
Because an old man chatters in the shade—
Will all be like a story you have read
In childhood and remembered for the pictures.
And when the best friend of your life goes down,
When first you know in him the slackening
That comes, and coming always tells the end,—
Now in a common word that would have passed
Uncaught from any other lips than his,
Now in some trivial act of every day,
Done as he might have done it all along
But for a twinging little difference
That nips you like a squirrel's teeth—oh, yes,
Then you will understand it well enough.
But oftener it comes in other ways;
It comes without your knowing when it comes;
You know that he is changing, and you know
That he is going—just as I know now
That Archibald is going, and that I
Am staying. . . . Look at me, my boy,
And when the time shall come for you to see
That I must follow after him, try then
To think of me, to bring me back again,
Just as I was to-day. Think of the place
Where we are sitting now, and think of me—
Think of old Isaac as you knew him then,

When you set out with him in August once
To see old Archibald."—The words come back
Almost as Isaac must have uttered them
And there comes with them a dry memory
Of something in my throat that would not move.

If you had asked me then to tell just why
I made so much of Isaac and the things
He said, I should have gone far for an answer;
For I knew it was not sorrow that I felt,
Whatever I may have wished it, or tried then
To make myself believe. My mouth was full
Of words, and they would have been comforting
To Isaac, spite of my twelve years, I think;
But there was not in me the willingness
To speak them out. Therefore I watched the ground;
And I was wondering what made the Lord
Create a thing so nervous as an ant,
When Isaac, with commendable unrest,
Ordained that we should take the road again—
For it was yet three miles to Archibald's,
And one to the first pump. I felt relieved
All over when the old man told me that;
I felt that he had stilled a fear of mine
That those extremities of heat and cold
Which he had long gone through with Archibald
Had made the man impervious to both;
But Isaac had a desert somewhere in him,
And at the pump he thanked God for all things
That He had put on earth for men to drink
And he drank well,—so well that I proposed
That we go slowly lest I learn too soon
The bitterness of being left behind,
And all those other things. That was a joke
To Isaac, and it pleased him very much;
And that pleased me—for I was twelve years old.

At the end of an hour's walking after that
The cottage of old Archibald appeared.
Little and white and high on a smooth round hill
It stood, with hackmatacks and apple-trees
Before it, and a big barn-roof beyond;
And over the place—trees, houses, fields and all—
Hovered an air of still simplicity
And a fragrance of old summers—the old style
That lives the while it passes. I dare say
That I was lightly conscious of all this
When Isaac, of a sudden, stopped himself,
And for the long first quarter of a minute
Gazed with incredulous eyes, forgetful quite
Of breezes and of me and of all else
Under the scorching sun but a smooth-cut field,
Faint yellow in the distance. I was young,
But there were a few things that I could see,
And this was one of them.—"Well, well!" said he;
And "Archibald will be surprised, I think,"
Said I. But all my childhood subtlety
Was lost on Isaac, for he strode along
Like something out of Homer—powerful
And awful on the wayside, so I thought.
Also I thought how good it was to be
So near the end of my short-legged endeavor
To keep the pace with Isaac for five miles.

Hardly had we turned in from the main road
When Archibald, with one hand on his back
And the other clutching his huge-headed cane,
Came limping down to meet us.—"Well! well! well!"
Said he; and then he looked at my red face,
All streaked with dust and sweat, and shook my hand,
And said it must have been a right smart walk
That we had had that day from Tilbury Town.—
"Magnificent," said Isaac; and he told
About the beautiful west wind there was

Which cooled and clarified the atmosphere.
"You must have made it with your legs, I guess,"
Said Archibald; and Isaac humored him
With one of those infrequent smiles of his
Which he kept in reserve, apparently,
For Archibald alone. "But why," said he,
"Should Providence have cider in the world
If not for such an afternoon as this?"
And Archibald, with a soft light in his eyes,
Replied that if he chose to go down cellar,
There he would find eight barrels—one of which
Was newly tapped, he said, and to his taste
An honor to the fruit. Isaac approved
Most heartily of that, and guided us
Forthwith, as if his venerable feet
Were measuring the turf in his own door-yard,
Straight to the open rollway. Down we went,
Out of the fiery sunshine to the gloom,
Grateful and half sepulchral, where we found
The barrels, like eight potent sentinels,
Close ranged along the wall. From one of them
A bright pine spile stuck out alluringly,
And on the black flat stone, just under it,
Glimmered a late-spilled proof that Archibald
Had spoken from unfeigned experience.
There was a fluted antique water-glass
Close by, and in it, prisoned, or at rest,
There was a cricket, of the brown soft sort
That feeds on darkness. Isaac turned him out,
And touched him with his thumb to make him jump,
And then composedly pulled out the plug
With such a practised hand that scarce a drop
Did even touch his fingers. Then he drank
And smacked his lips with a slow patronage
And looked along the line of barrels there
With a pride that may have been forgetfulness
That they were Archibald's and not his own.

"I never twist a spigot nowadays,"
He said, and raised the glass up to the light,
"But I thank God for orchards." And that glass
Was filled repeatedly for the same hand
Before I thought it worth while to discern
Again that I was young, and that old age,
With all his woes, had some advantages.
"Now, Archibald," said Isaac, when we stood
Outside again, "I have it in my mind
That I shall take a sort of little walk—
To stretch my legs and see what you are doing.
You stay and rest your back and tell the boy
A story: Tell him all about the time
In Stafford's cabin forty years ago,
When four of us were snowed up for ten days
With only one dried haddock. Tell him all
About it, and be wary of your back.
Now I will go along."—I looked up then
At Archibald, and as I looked I saw
Just how his nostrils widened once or twice
And then grew narrow. I can hear to-day
The way the old man chuckled to himself—
Not wholesomely, not wholly to convince
Another of his mirth,—as I can hear
The lonely sigh that followed.—But at length
He said: "The orchard now's the place for us;
We may find something like an apple there,
And we shall have the shade, at any rate."
So there we went and there we laid ourselves
Where the sun could not reach us; and I champed
A dozen of worm-blighted astrakhans
While Archibald said nothing—merely told
The tale of Stafford's cabin, which was good,
Though "master chilly"—after his own phrase—
Even for a day like that. But other thoughts
Were moving in his mind, imperative,
And writhing to be spoken: I could see

The glimmer of them in a glance or two,
Cautious, or else unconscious, that he gave
Over his shoulder: . . . "Stafford and the rest—
But that's an old song now, and Archibald
And Isaac are old men. Remember, boy,
That we are old. Whatever we have gained,
Or lost, or thrown away, we are old men.
You look before you and we look behind,
And we are playing life out in the shadow—
But that's not all of it. The sunshine lights
A good road yet before us if we look,
And we are doing that when least we know it;
For both of us are children of the sun,
Like you, and like the weed there at your feet,
The shadow calls us, and it frightens us—
We think; but there's a light behind the stars
And we old fellows who have dared to live,
We see it—and we see the other things,
The other things . . . Yes, I have seen it come
These eight years, and these ten years, and I know
Now that it cannot be for very long
That Isaac will be Isaac. You have seen—
Young as you are, you must have seen the strange
Uncomfortable habit of the man?
He'll take my nerves and tie them in a knot
Sometimes, and that's not Isaac. I know that—
And I know what it is: I get it here
A little, in my knees, and Isaac—here."
The old man shook his head regretfully
And laid his knuckles three times on his forehead.
"That's what it is: Isaac is not quite right.
You see it, but you don't know what it means:
The thousand little differences—no,
You do not know them, and it's well you don't;
You'll know them soon enough—God bless you, boy!—
You'll know them, but not all of them—not all.
So think of them as little as you can:

There's nothing in them for you, or for me—
But I am old and I must think of them;
I'm in the shadow, but I don't forget
The light, my boy,—the light behind the stars.
Remember that: remember that I said it;
And when the time that you think far away
Shall come for you to say it—say it, boy;
Let there be no confusion or distrust
In you, no snarling of a life half lived,
Nor any cursing over broken things
That your complaint has been the ruin of.
Live to see clearly and the light will come
To you, and as you need it.—But there, there,
I'm going it again, as Isaac says,
And I'll stop now before you go to sleep.—
Only be sure that you growl cautiously,
And always where the shadow may not reach you."

Never shall I forget, long as I live,
The quaint thin crack in Archibald's voice,
The lonely twinkle in his little eyes,
Or the way it made me feel to be with him.
I know I lay and looked for a long time
Down through the orchard and across the road,
Across the river and the sun-scorched hills
That ceased in a blue forest, where the world
Ceased with it. Now and then my fancy caught
A flying glimpse of a good life beyond—
Something of ships and sunlight, streets and singing,
Troy falling, and the ages coming back,
And ages coming forward: Archibald
And Isaac were good fellows in old clothes,
And Agamemnon was a friend of mine;
Ulysses coming home again to shoot
With bows and feathered arrows made another,
And all was as it should be. I was young.

So I lay dreaming of what things I would,
Calm and incorrigibly satisfied
With apples and romance and ignorance,
And the still smoke from Archibald's clay pipe.
There was a stillness over everything,
As if the spirit of heat had laid its hand
Upon the world and hushed it; and I felt
Within the mightiness of the white sun
That smote the land around us and wrought out
A fragrance from the trees, a vital warmth
And fullness for the time that was to come,
And a glory for the world beyond the forest.
The present and the future and the past,
Isaac and Archibald, the burning bush,
The Trojans and the walls of Jericho,
Were beautifully fused; and all went well
Till Archibald began to fret for Isaac
And said it was a master day for sunstroke.
That was enough to make a mummy smile,
I thought; and I remained hilarious,
In face of all precedence and respect,
Till Isaac (who had come to us unheard)
Found he had no tobacco, looked at me
Peculiarly, and asked of Archibald
What ailed the boy to make him chirrup so.
From that he told us what a blessed world
The Lord had given us.—"But, Archibald,"
He added, with a sweet severity
That made me think of peach-skins and goose-flesh,
"I'm half afraid you cut those oats of yours
A day or two before they were well set."
"They were set well enough," said Archibald,—
And I remarked the process of his nose
Before the words came out. "But never mind
Your neighbor's oats: you stay here in the shade
And rest yourself while I go find the cards.
We'll have a little game of seven-up

And let the boy keep count."—"We'll have the game,
Assuredly," said Isaac; "and I think
That I will have a drop of cider, also."

They marched away together towards the house
And left me to my childish ruminations
Upon the ways of men. I followed them
Down cellar with my fancy, and then left them
For a fairer vision of all things at once
That was anon to be destroyed again
By the sound of voices and of heavy feet—
One of the sounds of life that I remember,
Though I forget so many that rang first
As if they were thrown down to me from Sinai.

So I remember, even to this day,
Just how they sounded, how they placed themselves,
And how the game went on while I made marks
And crossed them out, and meanwhile made some Trojans.
Likewise I made Ulysses, after Isaac,
And a little after Flaxman. Archibald
Was injured when he found himself left out,
But he had no heroics, and I said so:
I told him that his white beard was too long
And too straight down to be like things in Homer.
"Quite so," said Isaac.—"Low," said Archibald;
And he threw down a deuce with a deep grin
That showed his yellow teeth and made me happy.
So they played on till a bell rang from the door,
And Archibald said, "Supper."—After that
The old men smoked while I sat watching them
And wondered with all comfort what might come
To me, and what might never come to me;
And when the time came for the long walk home
With Isaac in the twilight, I could see
The forest and the sunset and the sky-line,
No matter where it was that I was looking:

The flame beyond the boundary, the music,
The foam and the white ships, and two old men
Were things that would not leave me.—And that night
There came to me a dream—a shining one,
With two old angels in it. They had wings,
And they were sitting where a silver light
Suffused them, face to face. The wings of one
Began to palpitate as I approached,
But I was yet unseen when a dry voice
Cried thinly, with unpatronizing triumph,
"I've got you, Isaac; high, low, jack, and the game."

Isaac and Archibald have gone their way
To the silence of the loved and well-forgotten.
I knew them, and I may have laughed at them;
But there's a laughing that has honor in it,
And I have no regret for light words now.
Rather I think sometimes they may have made
Their sport of me;—but they would not do that,
They were too old for that. They were old men,
And I may laugh at them because I knew them.

Archibald's Example

OLD Archibald, in his eternal chair,
Where trespassers, whatever their degree,
Were soon frowned out again, was looking off
Across the clover when he said to me:

"My green hill yonder, where the sun goes down
Without a scratch, was once inhabited
By trees that injured him—an evil trash
That made a cage, and held him while he bled.

"Gone fifty years, I see them as they were
Before they fell. They were a crooked lot
To spoil my sunset, and I saw no time
In fifty years for crooked things to rot.

"Trees, yes; but not a service or a joy
To God or man, for they were thieves of light.
So down they came. Nature and I looked on,
And we were glad when they were out of sight.

"Trees are like men, sometimes; and that being so,
So much for that." He twinkled in his chair,
And looked across the clover to the place
That he remembered when the trees were there.

Recalled

LONG after there were none of them alive
About the place—where there is now no place
But a walled hole where fruitless vines embrace
Their parent skeletons that yet survive
In evil thorns—none of us could arrive
At a more cogent answer to their ways
Than one old Isaac in his latter days
Had humor or compassion to contrive.

I mentioned them, and Isaac shook his head:
"The Power that you call yours and I call mine
Extinguished in the last of them a line
That Satan would have disinherited.
When we are done with all but the Divine,
We die." And there was no more to be said.

Stafford's Cabin

ONCE there was a cabin here, and once there was a man;
And something happened here before my memory began.
Time has made the two of them the fuel of one flame
And all we have of them is now a legend and a name.

All I have to say is what an old man said to me,
And that would seem to be as much as there will ever be.
"Fifty years ago it was we found it where it sat."—
And forty years ago it was old Archibald said that

"An apple tree that's yet alive saw something, I suppose,
Of what it was that happened there, and what no mortal knows.
Some one on the mountain heard far off a master shriek,
And then there was a light that showed the way for men to seek.

"We found it in the morning with an iron bar behind,
And there were chains around it; but no search could ever find,
Either in the ashes that were left, or anywhere,
A sign to tell of who or what had been with Stafford there.

"Stafford was a likely man with ideas of his own—
Though I could never like the kind that likes to live alone;
And when you met, you found his eyes were always on your shoes,
As if they did the talking when he asked you for the news.

"That's all, my son. Were I to talk for half a hundred years
I'd never clear away from there the cloud that never clears.
We buried what was left of it,—the bar, too, and the chains;
And only for the apple tree there's nothing that remains."

Forty years ago it was I heard the old man say,
"That's all, my son."—And here again I find the place to-day,
Deserted and told only by the tree that knows the most,
And overgrown with golden-rod as if there were no ghost.

The Sheaves

WHERE long the shadows of the wind had rolled,
Green wheat was yielding to the change assigned;
And as by some vast magic undivined
The world was turning slowly into gold.
Like nothing that was ever bought or sold
It waited there, the body and the mind;
And with a mighty meaning of a kind
That tells the more the more it is not told.

So in a land where all days are not fair,
Fair days went on till on another day
A thousand golden sheaves were lying there,
Shining and still, but not for long to stay—
As if a thousand girls with golden hair
Might rise from where they slept and go away.

New England

Here where the wind is always north-north-east
And children learn to walk on frozen toes,
Wonder begets an envy of all those
Who boil elsewhere with such a lyric yeast
Of love that you will hear them at a feast
Where demons would appeal for some repose,
Still clamoring where the chalice overflows
And crying wildest who have drunk the least.

Passion is here a soilure of the wits,
We're told, and Love a cross for them to bear;
Joy shivers in the corner where she knits
And Conscience always has the rocking-chair,
Cheerful as when she tortured into fits
The first cat that was ever killed by Care.

V

AGAINST THE SKY

"I am sorry that I have painted myself in such lugubrious colors. The world is not a 'prison house' but a kind of spiritual kindergarten, where millions of bewildered infants are trying to spell God with the wrong blocks."

The Man Against the Sky

BETWEEN me and the sunset, like a dome
Against the glory of a world on fire,
Now burned a sudden hill,
Bleak, round, and high, by flame-lit height made higher,
With nothing on it for the flame to kill
Save one who moved and was alone up there
To loom before the chaos and the glare
As if he were the last god going home
Unto his last desire.

Dark, marvelous, and inscrutable he moved on
Till down the fiery distance he was gone,
Like one of those eternal, remote things
That range across a man's imaginings
When a sure music fills him and he knows
What he may say thereafter to few men,—
The touch of ages having wrought
An echo and a glimpse of what he thought
A phantom or a legend until then;
For whether lighted over ways that save,
Or lured from all repose,
If he go on too far to find a grave,
Mostly alone he goes.

Even he, who stood where I had found him,
On high with fire all round him,
Who moved along the molten west,
And over the round hill's crest
That seemed half ready with him to go down,
Flame-bitten and flame-cleft,
As if there were to be no last thing left
Of a nameless unimaginable town,—
Even he who climbed and vanished may have taken
Down to the perils of a depth not known,

From death defended though by men forsaken,
The bread that every man must eat alone;
He may have walked while others hardly dared
Look on to see him stand where many fell;
And upward out of that, as out of hell,
He may have sung and striven
To mount where more of him shall yet be given,
Bereft of all retreat,
To sevenfold heat,—
As on a day when three in Dura shared
The furnace, and were spared
For glory by that king of Babylon
Who made himself so great that God, who heard,
Covered him with long feathers, like a bird.

Again, he may have gone down easily,
By comfortable altitudes, and found,
As always, underneath him solid ground
Whereon to be sufficient and to stand
Possessed already of the promised land,
Far stretched and fair to see:
A good sight, verily,
And one to make the eyes of her who bore him
Shine glad with hidden tears.
Why question of his ease of who before him,
In one place or another where they left
Their names as far behind them as their bones,
And yet by dint of slaughter toil and theft,
And shrewdly sharpened stones,
Carved hard the way for his ascendency
Through deserts of lost years?
Why trouble him now who sees and hears
No more than what his innocence requires,
And therefore to no other height aspires
Than one at which he neither quails nor tires?
He may do more by seeing what he sees

Than others eager for iniquities;
He may, by seeing all things for the best,
Incite futurity to do the rest.

Or with an even likelihood,
He may have met with atrabilious eyes
The fires of time on equal terms and passed
Indifferently down, until at last
His only kind of grandeur would have been,
Apparently, in being seen.
He may have had for evil or for good
No argument; he may have had no care
For what without himself went anywhere
To failure or to glory, and least of all
For such a stale, flamboyant miracle;
He may have been the prophet of an art
Immovable to old idolatries;
He may have been a player without a part,
Annoyed that even the sun should have the skies
For such a flaming way to advertise;
He may have been a painter sick at heart
With Nature's toiling for a new surprise;
He may have been a cynic, who now, for all
Of anything divine that his effete
Negation may have tasted,
Saw truth in his own image, rather small,
Forbore to fever the ephemeral,
Found any barren height a good retreat
From any swarming street,
And in the sun saw power superbly wasted;
And when the primitive old-fashioned stars
Came out again to shine on joys and wars
More primitive, and all arrayed for doom,
He may have proved a world a sorry thing
In his imagining,
And life a lighted highway to the tomb.

Or, mounting with infirm unsearching tread,
His hopes to chaos led,
He may have stumbled up there from the past,
And with an aching strangeness viewed the last
Abysmal conflagration of his dreams,—
A flame where nothing seems
To burn but flame itself, by nothing fed;
And while it all went out,
Not even the faint anodyne of doubt
May then have eased a painful going down
From pictured heights of power and lost renown,
Revealed at length to his outlived endeavor
Remote and unapproachable forever;
And at his heart there may have gnawed
Sick memories of a dead faith foiled and flawed
And long dishonored by the living death
Assigned alike by chance
To brutes and hierophants;
And anguish fallen on those he loved around him
May once have dealt the last blow to confound him,
And so have left him as death leaves a child,
Who sees it all too near;
And he who knows no young way to forget
May struggle to the tomb unreconciled.
Whatever suns may rise or set
There may be nothing kinder for him here
Than shafts and agonies;
And under these
He may cry out and stay on horribly;
Or, seeing in death too small a thing to fear,
He may go forward like a stoic Roman
Where pangs and terrors in his pathway lie,—
Or, seizing the swift logic of a woman,
Curse God and die.

Or maybe there, like many another one
Who might have stood aloft and looked ahead,

Black-drawn against wild red,
He may have built, unawed by fiery gules
That in him no commotion stirred,
A living reason out of molecules
Why molecules occurred,
And one for smiling when he might have sighed
Had he seen far enough,
And in the same inevitable stuff
Discovered an odd reason too for pride
In being what he must have been by laws
Infrangible and for no kind of cause.
Deterred by no confusion or surprise
He may have seen with his mechanic eyes
A world without a meaning, and had room,
Alone amid magnificence and doom,
To build himself an airy monument
That should, or fail him in his vague intent,
Outlast an accidental universe—
To call it nothing worse—
Or, by the burrowing guile
Of Time disintegrated and effaced,
Like once-remembered mighty trees go down
To ruin, of which by man may now be traced
No part sufficient even to be rotten,
And in the book of things that are forgotten
Is entered as a thing not quite worth while.
He may have been so great
That satraps would have shivered at his frown,
And all he prized alive may rule a state
No larger than a grave that holds a clown;
He may have been a master of his fate,
And of his atoms,—ready as another
In his emergence to exonerate
His father and his mother;
He may have been a captain of a host,
Self-eloquent and ripe for prodigies,
Doomed here to swell by dangerous degrees,

And then give up the ghost.
Nahum's great grasshoppers were such as these,
Sun-scattered and soon lost.

Whatever the dark road he may have taken,
This man who stood on high
And faced alone the sky,
Whatever drove or lured or guided him,—
A vision answering a faith unshaken,
An easy trust assumed of easy trials,
A sick negation born of weak denials,
A crazed abhorrence of an old condition,
A blind attendance on a brief ambition,—
Whatever stayed him or derided him,
His way was even as ours;
And we, with all our wounds and all our powers,
Must each await alone at his own height
Another darkness or another light;
And there, of our poor self dominion reft,
If inference and reason shun
Hell, Heaven, and Oblivion,
May thwarted will (perforce precarious,
But for our conservation better thus)
Have no misgiving left
Of doing yet what here we leave undone?
Or if unto the last of these we cleave,
Believing or protesting we believe
In such an idle and ephemeral
Florescence of the diabolical,—
If, robbed of two fond old enormities,
Our being had no onward auguries,
What then were this great love of ours to say
For launching other lives to voyage again
A little farther into time and pain,
A little faster in a futile chase
For a kingdom and a power and a Race
That would have still in sight

A manifest end of ashes and eternal night?
Is this the music of the toys we shake
So loud,—as if there might be no mistake
Somewhere in our indomitable will?
Are we no greater than the noise we make
Along one blind atomic pilgrimage
Whereon by crass chance billeted we go
Because our brains and bones and cartilage
Will have it so?
If this we say, then let us all be still
About our share in it, and live and die
More quietly thereby.

Where was he going, this man against the sky?
You know not, nor do I.
But this we know, if we know anything:
That we may laugh and fight and sing
And of our transience here make offering
To an orient Word that will not be erased,
Or, save in incommunicable gleams
Too permanent for dreams,
Be found or known.
No tonic and ambitious irritant
Of increase or of want
Has made an otherwise insensate waste
Of ages overthrown
A ruthless, veiled, implacable foretaste
Of other ages that are still to be
Depleted and rewarded variously
Because a few, by fate's economy,
Shall seem to move the world the way it goes;
No soft evangel of equality,
Safe-cradled in a communal repose
That huddles into death and may at last
Be covered well with equatorial snows—
And all for what, the devil only knows—
Will aggregate an inkling to confirm

The credit of a sage or of a worm,
Or tell us why one man in five
Should have a care to stay alive
While in his heart he feels no violence
Laid on his humor and intelligence
When infant Science makes a pleasant face
And waves again that hollow toy, the Race;
No planetary trap where souls are wrought
For nothing but the sake of being caught
And sent again to nothing will attune
Itself to any key of any reason
Why man should hunger through another season
To find out why 'twere better late than soon
To go away and let the sun and moon
And all the silly stars illuminate
A place for creeping things,
And those that root and trumpet and have wings,
And herd and ruminate,
Or dive and flash and poise in rivers and seas,
Or by their loyal tails in lofty trees
Hang screeching lewd victorious derision
Of man's immortal vision.
Shall we, because Eternity records
Too vast an answer for the time-born words
We spell, whereof so many are dead that once
In our capricious lexicons
Were so alive and final, hear no more
The Word itself, the living word
That none alive has ever heard
Or ever spelt,
And few have ever felt
Without the fears and old surrenderings
And terrors that began
When Death let fall a feather from his wings
And humbled the first man?
Because the weight of our humility,
Wherefrom we gain

A little wisdom and much pain,
Falls here too sore and there too tedious,
Are we in anguish or complacency,
Not looking far enough ahead
To see by what mad couriers we are led
Along the roads of the ridiculous,
To pity ourselves and laugh at faith
And while we curse life bear it?
And if we see the soul's dead end in death,
Are we to fear it?
What folly is here that has not yet a name
Unless we say outright that we are liars?
What have we seen beyond our sunset fires
That lights again the way by which we came?
Why pay we such a price, and one we give
So clamoringly, for each racked empty day
That leads one more last human hope away,
As quiet fiends would lead past our crazed eyes
Our children to an unseen sacrifice?
If after all that we have lived and thought,
All comes to Nought,—
If there be nothing after Now,
And we be nothing anyhow,
And we know that,—why live?
'Twere sure but weaklings' vain distress
To suffer dungeons where so many doors
Will open on the cold eternal shores
That look sheer down
To the dark tideless floods of Nothingness
Where all who know may drown.

NOTES

IN his published and unpublished letters, Robinson occasionally made illuminating references to certain of his Tilbury Town poems, and the following notes are made up largely of quotations from these letters. For permission to make these quotations I wish to express my indebtedness and gratitude as follows: to Mrs. Ruth Robinson Nivison, representative of the Robinson heirs; to Mr. H. Bacon Collamore and to the Colby College Library for the use of a passage in an unpublished letter from Robinson to Miss Edith Brower concerning "Vickery's Mountain;" to Mr. Carl J. Weber and to the *Colby College Library Bulletin* for the use of a passage in a letter from Robinson to Mr. Weber concerning "The Whip;" to the Harvard College Library for the use of a passage in an unpublished letter from Robinson to Mr. George W. Latham, quoted in my "Introduction," and also for the use of a passage in an unpublished letter from Robinson to Mr. Arthur R. Gledhill, which has oblique bearing on "The Long Race"; to Mr. Denham Sutcliffe and to the Harvard University Press for the use of passages in six letters from Robinson to Mr. Harry de Forest Smith, published in *Untriangulated Stars;* to Mr. Charles Beecher Hogan and to the Yale University Press for the use of Robinson's letter concerning "New England," reprinted in *A Bibliography of Edwin Arlington Robinson;* to The Macmillan Company for the use of passages in two letters published in *Selected Letters of Edwin Arlington Robinson*.

p. ii: "DEAR FRIENDS"

This gently ironic and sarcastic sonnet was first published in Robinson's first (privately printed) book of poems, *The Torrent and the Night Before* (1896), while he was still living in Gardiner, Maine. Three years earlier, under date of October 1, 1893, he wrote to Harry de Forest Smith, "I have nothing in particular to say except that it is rather lonesome here without you, and on dark, dull Sundays like this I find it hard to be cheerful and optimistic, and everything else that a useful man should be in order to fill his place in nature to the satisfaction of himself and his dear friends who feel so much for his welfare. I am half afraid that my 'dear friends' here in Gardiner will be disappointed in me if I do not do something before long, but somehow I don't care half as much about the matter as I ought. One of my greatest misfortunes is the total inability to admire the so-called successful men who are pointed out to poor devils like me as examples for me to follow and revere. If Merchant A and Barrister B are put here as 'ensamples to mortals,' I am afraid that I shall always stand in the shadow as one of Omar's broken pots. I suspect that I am pretty much what I am, and that I am pretty much a damned fool in many ways; but I further suspect that I am not altogether an ass, whatever my neighbors may say. I may live to see this egotistical idea exploded, but until that time comes I am to hug my own particular phantoms and think as I like. If I turn out a failure after all, and go hopelessly to the devil, I shall have Aldrich's lines to console myself with:

> Then if at last thine airy structure fall,
> Dissolve, and vanish, take myself to blame:
> They fail, and they alone, who have not striven."

(Denham Sutcliffe, editor, *Untriangulated Stars,* Cambridge, Harvard University Press, 1947, p. 107.)   The sarcasm and irony implicit in Robinson's ambiguous quotation from Thomas Bailey Aldrich, there, is best understood if this letter to Smith is read in conjunction with Robinson's letter to Latham (dated Dec. 20, 1893), quoted in part on p. xv of my "Introduction."

p. 1: "CAPTAIN CRAIG"
The rhymed aphorism from "Captain Craig" may serve as a reminder that for various reasons not all of the Tilbury Town poems have been collected in this volume. Too long to be included here, "Captain Craig" may be found in the *Collected Poems* (1937), pp. 113–169.

p. 8: "OLD KING COLE"
The seemingly ironic contrasts which Robinson establishes, here, between this Tilbury Town oddity and the "merry old soul" in the Mother Goose rhyme and also between this oddity and Coleridge's king who decreed a stately pleasure dome, are pertinent: this oddity will not permit his own personal griefs and disappointments to blacken and ruin the larger significance of his own life. The pivotal concept may be found in the last four lines of the seventh octave, beginning, "Though mine. . ." Notice also the paraphrase of John 4:32 in the line, "I may have meat you know not of."

p. 14: "LOST ANCHORS"
Perhaps the "warped" old sailor established an obvious parallel (or "manifest analogy") between the two stories he told; but Robinson requires the

reader to play with possible extensions of meaning. Try these suggestions. The basic analogy, implicit in the symbolic title, would seem to be that the old sailor had started his life-voyage with a cargo of spiritual and moral "anchors" which he regrets having lost, long ago. Robinson's repeated and extensive usage of Christian symbolism, in many of the Tilbury Town poems, may be cited as justification for wondering whether he here intended to invoke certain "mystical" extensions of meaning with the anchor image. For his own use of the words "mysticism" and "mystical" in a similar connection, see the notes on "John Evereldown" and on "The House on the Hill," below.

p. 15: "FRAGMENT"

Here is another tantalizingly "inferential" poem which seems to have "mystical" overtones. The central situation is this: the narrator impressionistically describes the fine but abandoned house where the wealthy Briony once lived. Where Briony went, or why he went, we are not told. Implicitly, the poem would seem to invoke, once again, the favorite Robinsonian antithesis between material values and spiritual values. Briony, having achieved material success, turned his back on it: "he knew too much for the life he led." If Briony said, "There are still some gods to please. And houses are built without hands, we're told," he was apparently paraphrasing II Corinthians 5:1: "For we know that if our earthly house of this tabernacle were dissolved, we have a building of God, an house not made with hands, eternal in the heavens." The remainder of II Corinthians 5 is pertinent to the apparent meaning of this poem; namely, that Briony turned his back on material values in order to realize spiritual values. I suggest, however, that the first octave must have a typographical error in the fifth line, as it occurs in *The Man Against the Sky* (1916) and in the *Collected Poems*: "Now many a man . . ." Briony is represented as an exception: *not* many a man would have done what he did. So that word "now" does not seem to me to make sense, and I have taken the liberty of changing it to "not."

p. 21: "THE LONG RACE"

The title phrase seems to me to be illuminated not only by a certain weather-vane race-horse Robinson used to admire from his bedroom window in Gardiner, Maine, but also by a sentence or two in an unpublished letter he wrote to his former high-school classmate Arthur Gledhill on Dec. 26, 1894: "Sometimes I wonder if I am not a damned fool after all, and feel very queer as I watch my old friends all going by me in the race. Perhaps my turn is coming—I rather think it is." (Manuscript letter, Houghton Library, Harvard College.)

p.26: "Bokardo"

Notice that Robinson achieves an added symbolism here, by naming this imagined character after a mathematician. See Robinson's allusion to Bokardo in his letter to George W. Latham, quoted on p. xv of my "Introduction."

p. 33: "Theophilus"

Notice the irony implicit in giving this devilish creature a name which means "Lover of God." See Luke's dedication in Luke 1:3.

p. 34: "Uncle Ananias"

Anyone familiar with Acts 5:1-6 will enjoy the appropriateness of this name Ananias, here.

p. 36: "Siege Perilous"

In the little action, here, this unnamed but Galahad-like character is represented as choosing a course of action which runs counter to the accepted materialistic values of the Tilbury Town group. Robinson heightens the irony by describing the action from the viewpoint of the group, thus suggesting that from a prudently materialistic viewpoint such an action must be considered sinful and wicked. But the total context of the poem represents the action of the central character as a profoundly spiritual and idealistic dedication to the highest truth, or to the "Light." Thus the "failure" exists not in the central character but rather in the limited vision of those who criticize the central character.

The metaphorical use of imagery borrowed from the Grail legend, here, anticipates the following passage in Part Seven of Robinson's *Merlin*:

> "No," Dagonet replied; "there was a Light;
> And Galahad, in the Siege Perilous,
> Alone of all on whom it fell, was calm;
> There was a Light wherein men saw themselves
> In one another as they might become—
> Or so they dreamed."

p.38: "Richard Cory"

Too often "pickled in anthological brine," as Robinson phrased it, this poem has frequently been misinterpreted as evidence of the poet's all-pervading pessimism. The larger context of the Tilbury Town poems suggests that Robinson's interest, here, was to illuminate the ironic contrast between appearances and actualities, as applied to our inability to look behind the mask of human consciousness. Shortly before writing "Richard Cory," Robinson wrote to Smith, "Solitude is the best means of getting acquainted with one's self, but if one gets too well acquainted there is likely to be trouble. Sometimes we get sick of ourselves and that's bad. . . . There's a good deal to live for, but a man has to go through hell really to find it out. . . . Frank Avery blew his bowels out with a shot-gun. That was hell. I suppose you read about it in the paper." (*Untriangulated Stars*, p. 285.)

Also pertinent is an earlier letter to Smith, dated Feb. 3, 1897: "The *Bookman* evidently takes me for a yelling pessimist, and I must say that I am very much surprised. And the *Bookman* is not alone, either . . . a man in Denver, Colorado, thinks I have blue devils, but I assure you I have not. I also make free to say that many of my verses were written with a conscious hope that they might make some despairing devil a little stronger and a little better satisfied with things—not as they are, but as they are to be. This is the point the critics will not see. Because I don't dance on an illuminated hilltop and sing about bobolinks and bumble-bees, they tell me my world is a 'prison house' . . ." (*Untriangulated Stars*, p. 273). Part of Robinson's answer to the *Bookman* critic is quoted on p. 121 above.

p. 40: "Vickery's Mountain"

The context provided by the other poems helps us to avoid the danger of misinterpreting this poem. Yet, aware of Robinson's preoccupation with the conflict between idealism and materialism, in Tilbury Town, we might mistakenly view the image of "gold" in this poem as representing material wealth: so Vickery's response to the "gold" might be evaluated in terms of his dignified refusal to be interested in merely materialistic forms of gain. If, on the other hand, the image of "gold" be considered in a mystical sense as representing that kind of spiritual wealth so frequently represented by Robinson in his usage of the "Light" image, Vickery's response might be construed as representing his refusal to be interested in any spiritual values.

With these two possibilities of interpretation in mind—two diametrically opposed meanings—consider Robinson's own comments. To L. N. Chase he wrote on July 11, 1917, ". . . 'Vickery's Mountain' . . . is after all merely a study of human inertia, which is in Vickery's case something stronger than he is." (*Selected Letters of Edwin Arlington Robinson*, New York, Macmillan, p. 104.) To another correspondent, Miss Edith Brower, Robinson wrote on March 15, 1914: "Others have had . . . trouble with Vickery, trying to read into it all manner of stuff, when I merely meant that the gold was waiting for him, but the Fates and devils wouldn't allow him to accumulate sufficient sense and energy to go and get it. Maybe there is so much of Vickery in all of us that we don't recognize him when he is set before us." (Manuscript letter, H. Bacon Collamore Collection of Robinson books and manuscripts, Colby College Library.)

p. 42: "The Tree in Pamela's Garden"

Again, in the context of the other Tilbury Town poems, this poem achieves certain "mystical" extensions of meaning. Misunderstood by her neighbors as alone and lonely, Pamela is honored by the poet because she has fixed her love on values which transcend the love of woman for man. Pamela, like Old King Cole, might well paraphrase John 4:32 in saying to her neighbors, "I have food to eat that ye know not of."

p. 48: "REUBEN BRIGHT"

Robinson's ability to enjoy the ridiculous, even at his own expense, was strong enough to let him relish an excruciating typographical error which crept into the first printing of the last line of "Reuben Bright," in the *Collected Poems*. It was a meaningful error, in that it substituted slang for symbolic action, and created an entirely false effect, through the addition of the word "to," thus:

> ". . . and tore down to the slaughter house."

p. 52: "THE GIFT OF GOD"

On July 11, 1917, Robinson wrote to L. N. Chase, "Whatever merit my work may or may not possess, I fancy that it will always be a waste of time for any reader who has not a fairly well developed sense of humor—which, as someone has said before, is a very serious thing—to bother with it. When I tell you that my poem called 'The Gift of God' has been interpreted as a touching tribute to our Saviour, you will require no further comment upon this point."

p. 55: "THE COMPANION"

Notice that while the title image would seem to hint obliquely at the object of the husband's infidelity, another important "companion" here is doubt.

p. 56: "THE CLINGING VINE"

Again the title suggests the basic irony of situation: the man who married a woman who seemed like a "clinging vine" discovers (after he has been unfaithful to her) that she now clings only to an ideal of what their love could have been. As the woman upbraids the man for having repudiated that ideal, her oblique and unintentional self-characterization becomes of far more interest than the mere triangle-situation.

p. 60: "LLEWELLYN AND THE TREE"

The central action here gives an ironic twist of meaning to the Garden of Eden allusion implicit in the title and explicit in the next-to-last stanza. Compare this with a similar usage in the poem entitled "The Tree in Pamela's Garden."

p. 70: "LUKE HAVERGAL"

Here is another tantalizingly "inferential" poem which seems to me best understood if considered as a dramatization of a psychological and psychopathic state of suicidal self-delusion, evoked by the man's grief over the death of his beloved. It would seem that Luke Havergal thinks he hears his beloved calling, and telling him to kill himself, so that he may join her in death. In this sense, "the western gate" serves not only as a fairly conventional symbol of death but also as a fairly unconventional symbol of suicide, which seems to Luke Havergal to be justified. Robinson mentioned the poem in a letter to Smith, written on Dec. 14, 1895: "I also have a piece of deliberate degeneration called 'Luke Havergal,' which is not at all funny." (*Untriangulated Stars*, p. 238.)

p. 75: "AMARYLLIS"

In the pastoral tradition of poetry, "Amaryllis" is the name which usually represents the type of the perfect or ideal woman, frequently with spiritual or mystical and platonic extensions of meaning. Here, Robinson establishes a wistful and ironic antithesis between the *death* of Amaryllis and the *life* of the modern, materialistic age, symbolized by Tilbury Town.

p. 82: "THE WHIP"

For one possible interpretation of this poem, see my "Introduction," pp. xii–xiii. Support for that interpretation might be made by noticing that the final octave begins with a line ("There were some ropes of sand Recorded long ago . . .") which would seem to suggest an implicit analogy between the total action of this poem and the total meaning of a pertinent stanza which contains an allusion to "thy rope of sands" in George Herbert's famous poem, "The Collar:"

> Forsake thy cage,
> Thy rope of sands,
> Which petty thoughts have made, and made to thee
> Good cable, to enforce and draw
> And be thy law,
> While thou didst wink and wouldst not see.

Robinson made at least one comment on "The Whip," in a letter he wrote to Mr. Carl J. Weber, on Jan. 28, 1923: "I hardly know what to say about "The Whip," except that it is supposed to be a literal and not a figurative instrument. In this poem—not to mention a few others—I may have gone a little too far and given the reader too much to carry. If he refuses to carry it, perhaps I have only myself to blame. . . ." (Printed in *Saturday Review of Literature*, April 17, 1943, p. 54.)

p. 87: "Leonora"

Compare the implicit attitude toward death, here, with that expressed by Robinson to Smith in a letter dated March 15, 1897, concerning the death of his mother: ". . . I can't quite understand—yet—the laws of compensation that make a woman suffer what she did and from so many causes. We say she died of diphtheria. What does that mean? It means just this: she had endured all she could and was ready to die. I had been watching it for a year. If she had not had diphtheria, or membranous croup, or whatever it was that took her off so hellishly, she would have gone crazy." (*Untriangulated Stars*, p. 279.)

p. 88: "How Annandale Went Out"

One particular example of "euthanasia" practised by a doctor occurred in Robinson's own home; but with an ironic twist, in that it was self-inflicted. Robinson's brother Dean, who was a doctor, apparently used a needle to give himself a lethal "shot" of morphine, which was believed to have caused his death.

The earliest (and chronologically the first) Annandale poem, entitled "The Book of Annandale," was considered too long to be included here with these other two Annandale poems. The gist of "The Book of Annandale" may be found summarized in "Annandale Again"; it may be found entire in *Collected Poems*, pp. 195–211.

p. 96: "Supremacy"

Throughout this third group of Tilbury Town poems, Robinson has been exploring the difference between material failure and spiritual failure; the difference between apparent spiritual failure and actual spiritual triumph. "Supremacy" may serve as a fitting summary of this group of poems. In a letter to Smith, dated Oct. 1, 1893, Robinson discussed "Supremacy" thus:

"My fancy gets a little lively in those fourteen lines. I have never been quite able to know what to make of them. They may be nothing but rot—they surely are if the reader can make nothing of them—but I have always cherished the idea that there is a thought mixed up in them that is worth the trouble of the thinking. . . . It really seems to me that I have brought out the idea of the occasional realization of the questionable supremacy of ourselves over those we most despise in a moderate new way. If there is a little poetry in it, then all the better. There is poetry in all types of humanity—even in lawyers and horse-jockeys—if we are willing to search it out; and I have tried to find a little for the poor fellows in my hell, which is an exceedingly worldly and transitory one, before they soar above me in my ignorance of what is, to sing in the sun—not in triumph over me, but in the glad truth that destiny has worked out for them." (*Untriangulated Stars*, pp. 108–109.)

p. 99: "John Evereldown"

Robinson's experiments with ballad forms began before the appearance of his first book, *The Torrent and the Night Before* (1896). In a letter to Smith, dated Oct. 7, 1894, he explained that he was working on some "tavern songs" which would be "musical enough in themselves to be songs first and poems after," and yet would also have "a little mysticism" in them. Although there may seem to be precious little mysticism in "John Evereldown," it is possible to take the word "light" metaphorically, and in the conventional sense of Biblical symbolism. In this connection, see the note on "Archibald's Example," below.

p. 101: "The House on the Hill"

I believe there is justification for finding two distinct levels of meaning in this poem: a physical or material level, and a spiritual level. Robinson himself gave some encouragement to such a possibility, in a letter to Smith, under date of Feb. 25, 1894, where he enclosed an early draft of the poem, bearing as subtitle, "Villanelle of Departure," with its overtones not merely of going away from a house but also of going out of life, into death and beyond. The letter to Smith reads in part as follows: "I have felt well enough bodily but I have been in a bad mood. Yesterday I partially drove it off by making a rondeau and a villanelle. The latter is a little mystical perhaps and is an attempt to show the poetry of the commonplace. Here it is,—you may judge for yourself." (*Untriangulated Stars*, p. 132.)

The specific imagery of the poem represents a house that has been abandoned; a house in which there is "ruin and decay." By extension, symbolically, the image might be taken as representing a human body from which all the attributes of life have departed, or it might be taken as representing a graveyard, which is a "House of Death," from which the spirit has departed. Compare this poetic use of the "house" image with a related use in "Leonora," page 87, above.

p. 116: "Archibald's Example"

The central thought in these five quatrains—the underlying thought illuminated by the symbolic action—seems to turn on the phrase, "thieves of light." Compare Archibald's remark in "Isaac and Archibald," beginning,

> I'm in the shadow, but I don't forget
> The light, my boy,—the light behind the stars.

Throughout his poetry, or at least throughout most of his poetry, Robinson showed such partiality for the traditional Christian symbolism implicit in the "light" image that he sometimes overworked it.

141

p. 120: "New England"

Strictly speaking, this sonnet does not belong with the Tilbury Town poems, and yet it should be able to find a comfortable place on the "Edge of Town." It certainly is not an excellent sonnet; but it is good enough to be included here because Robinson's own comment on it calls particular attention to the difficulties of using irony—which never got him into deeper trouble than when he wrote "New England." Its magazine-appearance in the (London) *Outlook* for Nov. 3, 1923 (Vol. LII, p. 335), soon noticed in the United States, brewed a teapot-tempest. Many scolding critics misinterpreted it as evidence that Robinson had turned against his heritage and they claimed that he was sneering at New England. Back in Gardiner, Maine, a local poet answered him in both prose and verse. Reluctantly, defensively, Robinson replied. His letter to the editor of *The Gardiner Journal* was printed on St. Valentine's Day, 1924:

". . . Having read Mr. D's vigorous letter and still more vigorous poem in the *Journal* of last week, I find myself constrained to ask for a small amount of space in which to say a few words of explanation. If Mr. D. will be good enough to give my unfortunate sonnet one more reading, and if he will observe that Intolerance, used ironically, is the subject of the first sentence . . . he will see that the whole thing is a satirical attack not upon New England but upon the same patronizing pagans whom he flays with such vehemence in his own poem. As a matter of fact, I cannot quite see how the first eight lines of my sonnet are to be regarded as even intelligible if read in any other way than as an oblique attack upon all those who are forever throwing dead cats at New England for its alleged emotional and moral frigidity. As for the last six lines, I should suppose that the deliberate insertion of 'It seems' would be enough to indicate the key in which they are written. Apparently Mr. D. has fallen into the not uncommon error of seizing upon certain words and phrases without pausing to consider just why and how they are used. Interpretation of one's own irony is always a little distressing, yet in this instance, it appears to be rather necessary. If this leaves Mr. D. still in doubt, it may be assumed that I have written an unusually bad sonnet—which is quite possible. . . ." (Quoted in Charles Beecher Hogan, *A Bibliography of Edwin Arlington Robinson*, New Haven, Yale University Press, 1936, pp. 179–180.) In the revised version of the poem, here used, the word "intolerance" was carefully avoided.

p. 123: "The Man Against the Sky"

After Amy Lowell had publicly described this poem as "pessimistic" in its tone and meaning, Robinson wrote to her, under date of March 8, 1916:

". . . I must hasten to correct, or try to correct, what seems to be a false impression on your part in regard to the last poem in the book. Nothing could have been farther from my mind when I wrote 'The Man' than any emissary of gloom or of despair. In the closing pages I meant merely, through what I supposed to be an obviously ironic medium, to carry materialism to its logical end and to indicate its futility as an explanation or a justification of existence. Perhaps you will read the poem again sometime and observe my 'lesson' in the last line. I thought of printing it in italics, but changed my mind since I don't like 'em." (*Selected Letters*, p. 93.)

The structural pattern of the poem depends on the initial image, the title image, only to the extent that the poet, not knowing who the figure is, may meditate on what kind of man he might be. Using this image, then, as a point of departure and return, Robinson develops a variety of possible attitudes toward human experience, including both the positive and the negative extremes. Even as early as the second stanza, however, the figure against the sky is considered as a possible emblem of the man of "vision." The many Biblical references and allusions are easily recognizable, throughout; but particular attention should be given to Robinson's recurrent use of "Word" in such a way as to echo John 1:1.

As late as January 7, 1932, Robinson wrote to an admirer of his poetry, "Perhaps 'The Man Against the Sky' comes as near as anything to representing my poetic vision—as you are good enough to call it." (Quoted in Edna Davis Romig, "Tilbury Town and Camelot," *University of Colorado Studies*, Vol. 19, No. 3 (1933), p. 318.)

INDEX

Aaron Stark	11	Leonora	87
Amaryllis	75	Llewellyn and the Tree	60
Annandale Again	89	Long Race, The	21
Another Dark Lady	65	Lost Anchors	14
Archibald's Example	116	Luke Havergal	70
Aunt Imogen	16	Man Against the Sky, The	123
Ben Trovato	51	Man in Our Town, A	73
Bewick Finzer	35	Mill, The	84
Bokardo	26	Miniver Cheevy	6
Cassandra	12	Mr. Flood's Party	102
Charles Carville's Eyes	76	New England	120
Cliff Klingenhagen	24	Old King Cole	8
Clinging Vine, The	56	Poor Relation, The	30
Companion, The	55	Rat, The	85
Dark House, The	22	Recalled	117
Eros Turannos	68	Reuben Bright	48
Exit	74	Richard Cory	38
Evangelist's Wife, An	39	Sheaves, The	119
Firelight	50	Siege Perilous	36
Flammonde	3	Souvenir	77
Fleming Helphenstine	25	Stafford's Cabin	118
For a Dead Lady	81	Story of the Ashes and the	
Fragment	15	Flame, The	45
Gift of God, The	52	Supremacy	96
Growth of "Lorraine", The	59	Tavern, The	100
Hector Kane	78	Theophilus	33
Her Eyes	46	Tree in Pamela's Garden, The	42
House on the Hill, The	101	Uncle Ananias	34
How Annandale Went Out	88	Unforgiven, The	66
Inferential	86	Vain Gratuities	54
Isaac and Archibald	104	Vickery's Mountain	40
Job the Rejected	49	Voice of Age, The	37
John Evereldown	99	Whip, The	82